How Computers Work

Second Edition

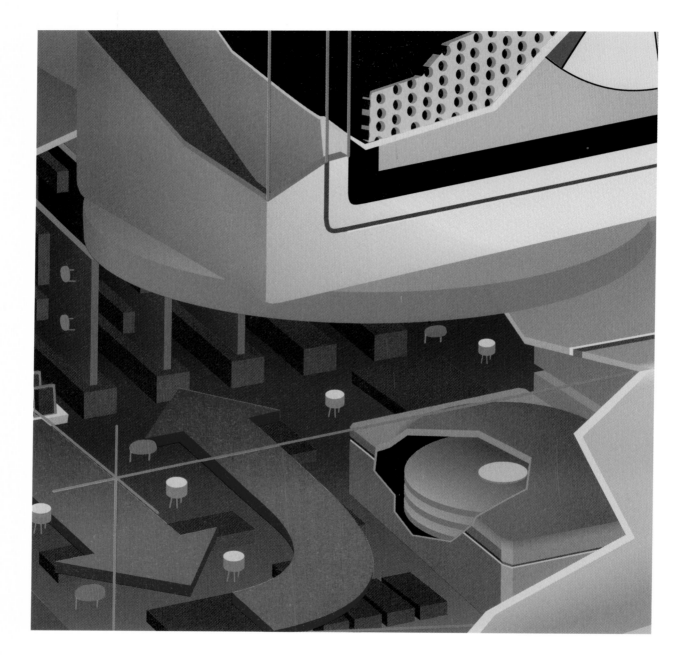

How Computers Work

Second Edition

Ron White

Illustrated by Timothy Edward Downs and Sarah Ishida

Ziff-Davis Press
Emeryville, California

Development Editors	Melinda E. Levine and Valerie Haynes Perry
Technical Reviewers	John Rizzo and Dick Hol
Project Coordinator	Ami Knox
Cover Design	Regan Honda
Cover Illustration	Mina Reimer
Book Design	Carrie English and Bruce Lundquist
Technical Illustration	Timothy Edward Downs and Sarah Ishida
Word Processing	Howard Blechman
Page Layout	Bruce Lundquist
Indexer	Kayla Sussell
Cover Copywriter	Valerie Haynes Perry

Ziff-Davis Press books are produced on a Macintosh computer system with the following applications: FrameMaker®, Microsoft® Word, QuarkXPress®, Adobe Illustrator®, Adobe Photoshop®, Adobe Streamline™, MacLink®*Plus*, Aldus® FreeHand™, Collage Plus™.

If you have comments or questions or would like to receive a free catalog, call or write:
Ziff-Davis Press
5903 Christie Avenue
Emeryville, CA 94608
800-688-0448

Published 1993. Second Edition 1995.

PART OF A CONTINUING SERIES

ISBN 1-56276-344-X

Manufactured in the United States of America

10 9 8 7 6 5 4 3 2 1

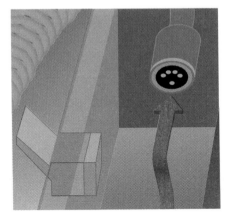

For Shannon and Michael,
who always kept me honest
in my explanations

"**How** It Works" debuted in *PC/Computing* in 1989 as part of a new section of the magazine called "Help." It would be nice if I could say we instantly knew the best way to create illustrated explanations of how computer components and software work. We didn't. For a long time, I've wanted to redo some of our earlier efforts. This book is that opportunity, and it lets me rearrange into some sort of sensible order the often random selection of topics that appeared in *PC/Computing*.

I had the privilege of launching "How It Works," but over the years, many people have worked on it, and I'm grateful for the research and explanations they've done. Deep thanks go to Herb Brody, Brett L. Glass, Preston Gralla, Christine Grech, Marty Jerome, Raymond Jones, Matthew Lake, Jack Nimersheim, Randy Ross, Stephen Sagman, Jan Smith, Dylan Tweney, Doug van Kirk, Mark L. Van Name and Bill Catchings, and Kenan Woods.

I'm also grateful to the dozens of people in the PC industry who've shared their knowledge, schematics, and white papers to make *How Computers Work* accurate. And thanks to *PC/Computing* who helped me handle my job at the magazine while this project was going on; to former Publisher Mike Edelhart, who started the ball rolling on this book; to Juliet Langley, Cindy Hudson, Melinda Levine, and Valerie Perry at ZD Press, who were always tolerant of my cavalier disregard for such niceties as outlines and chapter numbers; and to my assistant, Margaret Ficklen, for her invaluable help. And thanks to my wife, Sue, for her encouragement and her patience while waiting for me to pop out of writing mode. Finally, for this second edition, thanks to those readers who spotted inaccuracies in the first edition and took the trouble to write me.

I learned long ago that a writer's skill depends largely on how well the writer can borrow from others. In addition to the staffers and freelancers who've contributed to "How It Works," three books were invaluable for details on PC innards: *Inside the IBM PC* by Peter Norton, *The PC Configuration Handbook* by John Woram, and *The Winn Rosch Hardware Bible* by Winn Rosch. Also helpful was *The Way Things Work* by David Macaulay, not only for its own informative explanations of computers, but for its examples of how to combine text and art into clear explanations.

Finally, this book would not be what it is without the artwork of Timothy Edward Downs and Sarah Ishida. Invariably, they not only transformed my crude sketches into clear, informative illustrations, but also managed to make them into wonderful works of art.

Ron White
San Antonio

As I was finishing up the first edition of *How Computers Work*, I recall hurriedly inserting some paragraphs about technologies that were just making themselves known at that time—double-speed CD-ROM drives and local-bus video. Of course, we could have postponed publication of the first edition until I had time to cover these technical developments in depth. But that really wouldn't have solved the problem. By the time I had revised the first edition to include the new PC components, there would have been still newer technologies to write about. And if I'd delayed long enough to include those new technologies, there would have been still other new developments emerging from the labs of PC makers. It's a problem that never ends.

Clearly, it's only a problem to computer journalists trying to make their stories and books as timely as possible. For anyone else using computers, the rapid development of technology is a giant blessing. As soon as we run into a brick wall that limits what we can do with our computers, a new technology comes onto the scene to push back the wall. Local-bus data transfer, faster and bigger disk drives, and newer processors are just a few examples of this trend.

With computer generations measured in months rather than years, this, the second edition of *How Computers Work*, covers components that most people had not even dreamed of a couple of years ago. Many of these developments are so important that it's difficult to select the most significant ones. But surely near the top of the list are multimedia sound and video that have transformed CD-ROMs from carriers of merely large amounts of text and numbers to magical disks alive with sound, music, and moving images. This edition brings itself up to date with an entire section devoted to multimedia.

Other important developments that are new in this edition are the Internet, both VESA and PCI local-bus data transmission, and the Pentium processor. Additional new technologies are not as dramatic, but are important enough to have also found a place in this edition: floptical drives, dye-sublimation color printers, and jukebox CD-ROM drives.

As I finish this introduction, the last writing I'll do for this edition, I know that soon—possibly before the book reaches the book stores—there'll be something new I will wish I could have included. The P6 processor lurks in the nearby future, although I take comfort from the fact that it promises to be an evolutionary change from the Pentium processor, which itself was a revolutionary change from its predecessors. Telecommunications and the Internet are expanding at a rate that outdates nearly anything written about them. But the chapter here about the Internet will remain valid, if not comprehensive, for at least a few years. CD-ROM technology is changing even as I write, and I know that we'll soon have CDs that hold more data and are used interchangeably as sources of audio, video, and computer data. But right now there's a battle going on over how those CDs will hold data, and I can't hang around to see who's the winner.

I'd like to conclude with an excerpt from the first edition. The sentiments expressed then remain relevant and true.

Sorcerers have their magic wands—powerful, potentially dangerous tools with a life of their own. Witches have their familiars—creatures disguised as household beasts that could, if they choose, wreak the witches' havoc. Mystics have their golems—beings built of wood and tin brought to life to do their masters' bidding.

We have our personal computers.

PCs, too, are powerful creations that often seem to have a life of their own. Usually they respond to a seemingly magic incantation typed at a C:> prompt or to a wave of a mouse by performing tasks we couldn't imagine doing ourselves without some sort of preternatural help. But even as computers successfully carry out our commands, it's often difficult to quell the feeling that there's some wizardry at work here.

And then there are the times when our PCs, like malevolent spirits, rebel and open the gates of chaos onto our neatly ordered columns of numbers, our carefully wrought sentences, and our beautifully crafted graphics. When that happens, we're often convinced that we are, indeed, playing with power not entirely under our control. We become sorcerer's apprentices, whose every attempt to right things leads to deeper trouble.

Whether our personal computers are faithful servants or traitorous imps, most of us soon realize there's much more going on inside those putty-colored boxes than we really understand. PCs are secretive. Open their tightly sealed cases and you're confronted with poker-faced components. Few give any clues as to what they're about. Most of them consist of sphinxlike microchips that offer no more information about themselves than some obscure code printed on their impenetrable surfaces. The maze of circuit tracings etched on the boards is fascinating, but meaningless, hieroglyphics. Some crucial parts, such as the hard drive and power supply, are sealed with printed omens about the dangers of peeking inside, threats that put to shame the warnings on a pharaoh's tomb.

This book is based on two ideas. One is that the magic we understand is safer and more powerful than the magic we don't. This is not a hands-on how-to book. Don't look for any instructions for taking a screwdriver to this part or the other. But perhaps your knowing more about what's going on inside all those stoic components makes them all a little less formidable when something does go awry. The second idea behind this book is that knowledge, in itself, is a worthwhile and enjoyable goal. This book is written to respond to your random musings about the goings-on inside that box that you sit in front of several hours a day. If this book puts your questions to rest—or raises new ones—it will have done its job.

At the same time, however, I'm trusting that knowing the secrets behind the magician's legerdemain won't spoil the show. This is a real danger. Mystery is often as compelling as knowledge. I'd hate to think that anything you read in this book takes away that sense of wonder you have when you manage to make your PC do some grand, new trick. I hope that, instead, this book makes you a more confident sorcerer.

Despite all the tangible evidence of enhancements in hardware development, the following quote from the opening of the first edition still rings true:

Any sufficiently advanced technology is indistinguishable from magic.

—Arthur C. Clarke

Before You Begin

This book has been written with a certain type of personal computer in mind—the IBM PC-compatible computer, usually powered by an Intel microprocessor and most often running the MS-DOS operating system and Windows in one of its versions. Many of the specifics in these explanations apply only to that class of computer and those components.

In more general terms, the explanations also may apply to Macintosh computers, Unix workstations, and even minicomputers and mainframes. But I've made no attempt to devise universal explanations of how computers work. To do so would, of necessity, detract from the understanding that comes from inspecting specific components.

Even so, there is so much variety even within the IBM/Intel/MS-DOS world of PCs that, at times, I've had to limit my explanations to particular instances or stretch the boundaries of a particular situation to make an explanation as generic as possible. If you spot anything that doesn't seem quite right in this book, I pray that my liberties with the particulars are the only cause.

For now, I trust you'll enjoy this edition and find it informative. I'll see you again, I hope, in a few more years.

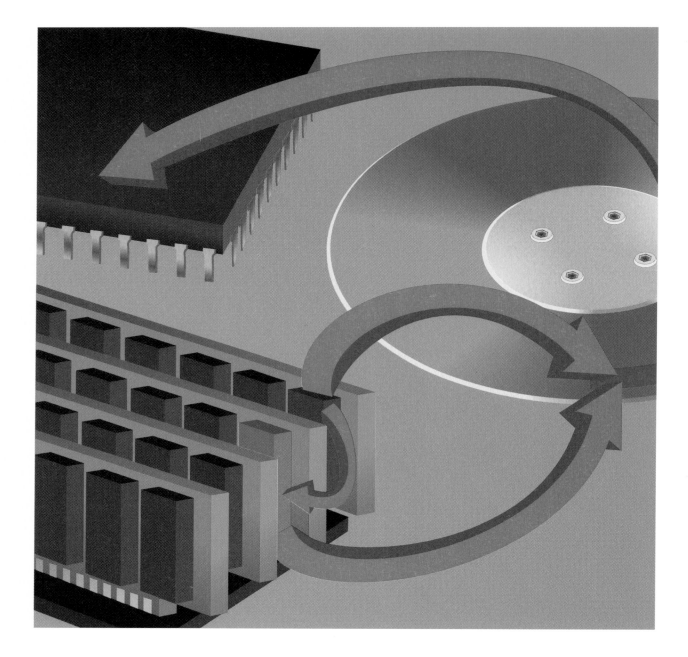

P A R T

BOOT-UP PROCESS

BEFORE your personal computer is turned on, it is a dead collection of
sheet metal, plastic, metallic tracings, and tiny flakes of silicon.
When you hit the On switch, one little burst of electricity—only about three to five volts—
starts a string of events that magically brings to life what otherwise would remain an
oversized paperweight.

Even with that spark of life in it, however, the PC is still rather stupid at first. It has
some primitive sense of self as it checks to see what parts are installed and working, like
those patients who've awakened from a coma and check to make sure that they have all
their arms and legs and that all their joints still work. But beyond taking inventory of itself,
the newly awakened PC still can't do anything really useful, certainly nothing we'd even
remotely think of as intelligent.

At best the newly awakened PC can search for intelligence—intelligence in the form of
an operating system that gives structure to the PC's primitive, amoebic existence. Then
comes a true education in the form of application software—programs that tell the PC how
to do tasks faster and more accurately than we could, a student who's outstripped its teacher.

But not all kinds of computers have to endure such a torturous rebirth each time
they're turned on. You encounter daily many computers that spring to life fully formed at
the instant they're switched on. You may not think of them as computers, but they are: cal-
culators, your car's electronic ignition, the timer in the microwave, and the unfathomable
programmer in your VCR. The difference between these and the big box on your desk is
hard wiring. Computers built to accomplish only one task—and they are very efficient about
doing that task—are hard-wired. But that means that they are more idiot savants than sages.

What makes your PC such a miraculous device is that each time you turn it on, it is a
tabula rasa, capable of doing anything your creativity—or, more usually, the creativity of
professional programmers—can imagine for it to do. It is a calculating machine, an artist's
canvas, a magical typewriter, an unerring accountant, and a host of other tools. To trans-
form it from one persona to another merely requires setting some of the microscopic
switches buried in the hearts of the microchips, a task accomplished by typing a command
or by clicking with your mouse on some tiny icon on the screen.

Such intelligence is fragile and short-lived. All those millions of microscopic switches are
constantly flipping on and off in time to dashing surges of electricity. All it takes is an errant
instruction or a stray misreading of a single switch to send this wonderful golem into a state
of catatonia. Or hit the Off switch and what was a pulsing artificial life dies without a whimper.

Then the next time you turn it on, birth begins all over again.

CHAPTER

1

How the Power-On Self-Test Works

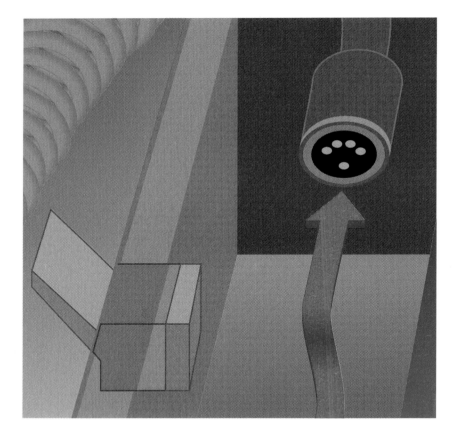

WHEN you hit your PC's On switch, nothing much seems to happen for several seconds. Actually, your computer is going through a complex set of operations to make sure all of its components are working properly and to warn you if something's amiss. This operation is the first step in an even more complicated process called the *boot-up* or simply, the *boot*. The term comes from the idea of lifting yourself up by your own bootstraps. In a PC, bootstrapping is necessary because the PC has to have some way of bringing all its components to life long enough so that they can accomplish the goal of loading an operating system. The operating system then takes on more complicated tasks that the boot code alone can't manage, including making the PC's hardware interact with software.

But before your PC can even attempt to load an operating system, it has to make sure that all the hardware components are running and that the CPU (central processing unit) and memory are functioning properly. This is the job of the *power-on self-test*, or POST.

The POST is the first thing your PC does when you turn it on, and it's your first warning of trouble with any of the components. When the POST detects an error from the display, memory, keyboard, or other basic components, it produces an error warning in the form of a message on your display and—in case your display is part of the problem—in the form of a series of beeps. Usually neither the beeps nor the on-screen message is specific enough to tell you exactly what is wrong. All they're intended to do is to point you in the general direction of the component that has a problem.

A single beep combined with a display of the normal DOS prompt means that all components have passed the POST. But any other combination of shorts beeps and long beeps usually means trouble. Even no beep at all indicates a problem.

Here's a table that tells how to translate the beeps—(•) for short, (−) for long—or lack of them.

Beeps	Display	Problem Area
None	None	Power
None	Cursor only	Power
None	DOS prompt	Speaker
•	DOS prompt	Normal
•	BASIC screen	Disk
• −	None	Monitor
• •	None	Monitor

Beeps	Display	Problem Area
• •	Error code	Other, usually memory
Several •	305 error code	Keyboard
Several •	Anything else	Power
Continuous beep	Anything else	Power
— •	Anything else	System board
— • •	Anything else	Monitor
— • • •	Anything else	Monitor

If no error message appears or beeps occur, however, that doesn't mean all the hardware components of your system are functioning as they should. The POST is capable of detecting only the most general types of errors. It can tell if a hard drive that's supposed to be installed isn't there, but it can't tell if there is trouble with the drive's formatting.

All in all, the POST does not appear to be extremely helpful. That's because most PCs function so reliably that only rarely does anything trigger a POST alarm. The POST's benefits are subtle but fundamental. Without it, you could never be sure of the PC's ability to carry out its tasks accurately and reliably.

Power-On Self-Test

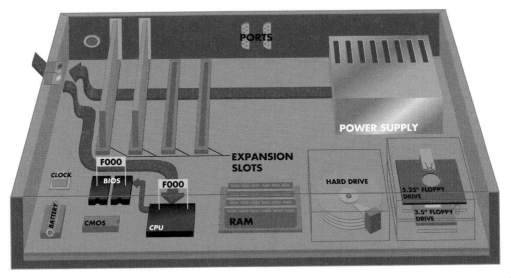

1 When you turn on your PC, an electrical signal follows a permanently programmed path to the CPU to clear leftover data from the chip's internal memory registers. The signal resets a CPU register called the program counter to a specific number. In the case of ATs and later computers, the hexadecimal number is F000. The number in the program counter tells the CPU the address of the next instruction that needs processing. In this case, the address is the beginning of a boot program stored permanently at the address F000 in a set of read-only memory (ROM) chips that contain the PC's basic input/output system (BIOS).

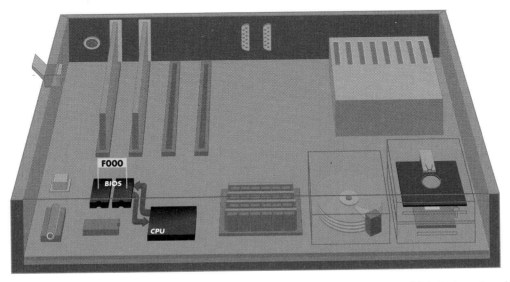

2 The CPU uses the address to find and invoke the ROM BIOS boot program, which in turn invokes a series of system checks, known as power-on self-tests, or POSTs. The CPU first checks itself and the POST program by reading code at various locations and checking it against identical permanent records.

[*Continued on next page.*]

Power-On Self-Test

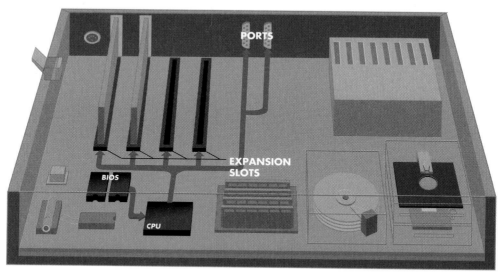

3 The CPU sends signals over the system *bus*—the circuits that connect all the components with each other—to make sure that they are all functioning.

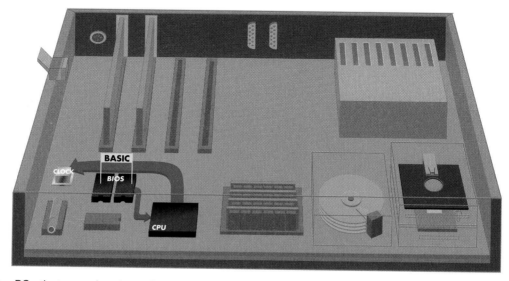

4 On older PCs that contain a kernel of the programming language BASIC in ROM, that section of code is checked while the CPU also checks the system's timer, which is responsible for making sure that all of the PC's operations function in a synchronized, orderly fashion.

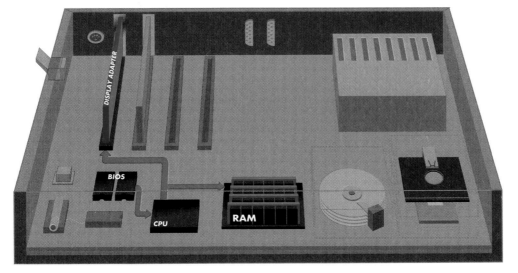

5 The POST procedure tests the memory contained on the display adapter and the video signals that control the display. It then makes the adapter's BIOS code a part of the system's overall BIOS and memory configuration. It's at this point that you'll first see something appear on your PC's monitor.

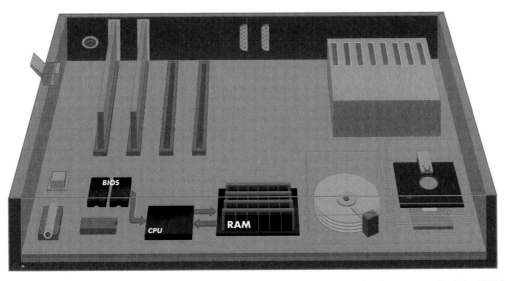

6 The POST runs a series of tests to ensure that the RAM chips are functioning properly. The CPU writes data to each chip, then reads it and compares what it reads with the data it sent to the chips in the first place. A running account of the amount of memory that's been checked is displayed on the monitor during this test. [*Continued on next page.*]

Power-On Self-Test

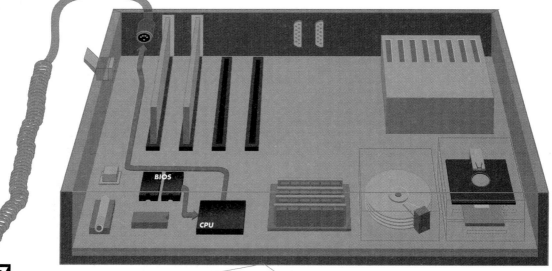

7 The CPU checks to make sure that the keyboard is attached properly and looks to see if any keys have been pressed.

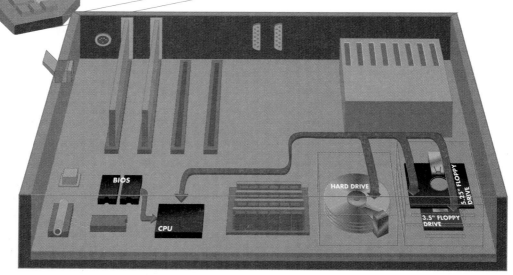

8 The POST sends signals over specific paths on the bus to any disk drives and listens for a response to determine what drives are available.

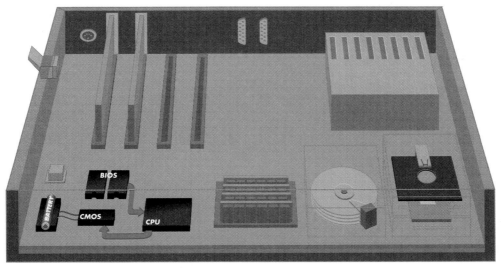

9 On AT class or later PCs, the results of the POST tests are compared with a record in a specific CMOS chip that is the official record of which components are installed. CMOS is a type of memory chip that retains its data when power is turned off as long as it receives a trickle of electricity from a battery. Any changes to the basic system configuration must be recorded in the CMOS setup data on all PCs that include that function. (Only the original PC and PC XT class of computers don't use a CMOS function.)

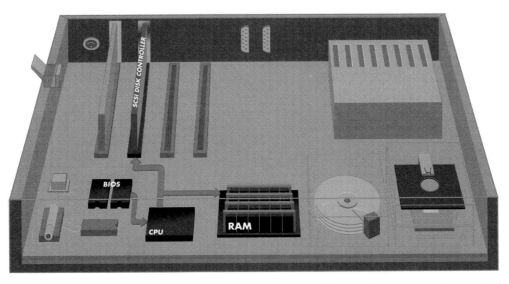

10 On systems that contain components that include their own BIOS, such as some disk controller cards, that BIOS code is recognized and incorporated as part of the system's own BIOS and memory use. Newer PCs may also run a Plug and Play operation to distribute system resources among different components. (See Chapter 3.) The PC is now ready to take the next step in the boot process: loading an operating system from disk.

C H A P T E R

2

How a Disk Boot Works

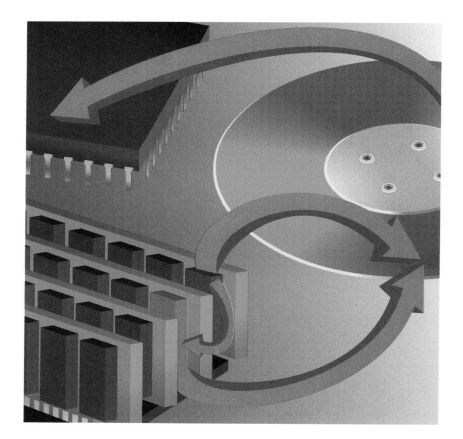

A personal computer can't do anything useful unless it's running an *operating system*—the software that lets the PC use other software. But before it can run an operating system, it needs some way to load the operating system from disk to random access memory (RAM). That way is with the *bootstrap* or simply, boot—a small amount of code that's permanently a part of the PC.

The bootstrap is aptly named because it lets the PC do something entirely on its own, without any outside operating system. Of course, the boot operation doesn't do very much. In fact, it has only two functions: one is to run a POST, or power-on self-test (described in the previous chapter), and the other is to search drives for an operating system. When these functions are complete, the boot operation launches the process of reading the operating system files and copying them to random access memory.

Why do PCs use such a roundabout arrangement? Why not simply make the operating system a part of the PC? A few low-end or specialized computers do this. Early computers used primarily for playing games, such as the Atari 400 and 800, and the recent Hewlett-Packard LX95 palmtop have a permanent operating system. The LX95 even includes an application program, Lotus 1-2-3, on a special microchip. But in most cases, the operating system is loaded from disk for two reasons.

It is simpler to upgrade the operating system when loading from a disk. When a company such as Microsoft—which makes MS-DOS and Windows 95, the most commonly used PC operating systems—wants to add new features or fix serious bugs, it can simply issue a new set of disks. Sometimes all that's necessary is a single file that patches a flaw in the operating system. It's cheaper for Microsoft to distribute an operating system on disk than to design a microchip that contains the operating system. And it's easier for computer users to install a new operating system from disk than it is to swap chips.

The other reason for loading an operating system from disk is that it gives users a choice of operating systems. Although most PCs based on microprocessors built by Intel use MS-DOS, there are alternative operating systems, such as Windows NT, Windows 95, OS/2, DR DOS, and Unix. In some PC set-ups, you can even choose which of the operating systems to use each time you turn on your computer. We'll use MS-DOS in the example shown here.

Disk Boot

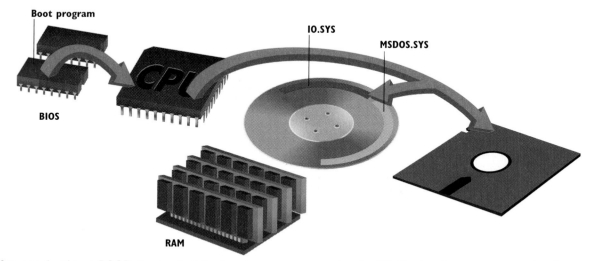

1 After conducting a POST check of all the hardware components of a PC, the boot program contained on the computer's ROM BIOS chips checks drive A to see if it contains a formatted floppy disk. If a disk is mounted in the drive, the program searches specific locations on the disk for the files that make up the first two parts of the operating system. You won't ordinarily see these system files because each is marked with a special file attribute that hides it from the DOS DIR command. For MS-DOS systems, the files are named IO.SYS and MSDOS.SYS. On IBM computers, the files are named IBMBIO.COM and IBMDOS.COM. If the floppy drive is empty, the boot program checks the hard drive C for the system files. If a boot disk does not contain the files, the boot program generates an error message.

2 After locating a disk with the system files, the boot program reads the data stored on the disk's first sector and copies that data to specific locations in RAM. This information constitutes the DOS *boot record*. The boot record is found in the same location on every formatted disk. The boot record is only about 512 bytes, just enough code to initiate the loading of the two hidden system files. After the BIOS boot program has loaded the boot record into memory at the hexadecimal address 7C00, the BIOS passes control to the boot record by branching to that address.

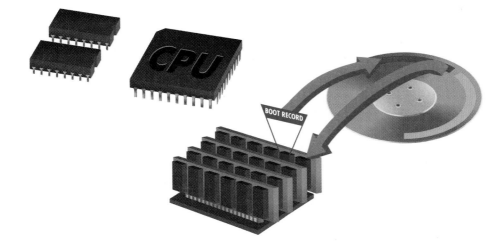

3 The boot record takes control of the PC and loads IO.SYS into RAM. The IO.SYS file contains extensions to the ROM BIOS and includes a routine called SYSINIT that manages the rest of the boot up. After loading IO.SYS, the boot record is no longer needed and is replaced in RAM by other code.

4 SYSINIT assumes control of the start-up process and loads MSDOS.SYS into RAM. The MSDOS.SYS file works with the BIOS to manage files, execute programs, and respond to signals from hardware.

[*Continued on next page.*]

Disk Boot

FILES=50
BUFFERS=20
DEVICE= HIMEM.SYS
DEVICE=RAMDRIVE.SYS

CONFIG.SYS

5 Under DOS, SYSINIT searches the root directory of the boot disk for a file named CONFIG.SYS. If CONFIG.SYS exists, SYSINIT tells MSDOS.SYS to execute the commands in the file. CONFIG.SYS is a file created by the user. Its commands tell the operating system how to handle certain operations, such as how many files may be opened at one time. CONFIG.SYS may also contain instructions to load device drivers. *Device drivers* are files containing code that extends the capabilities of the BIOS to control memory or hardware devices.

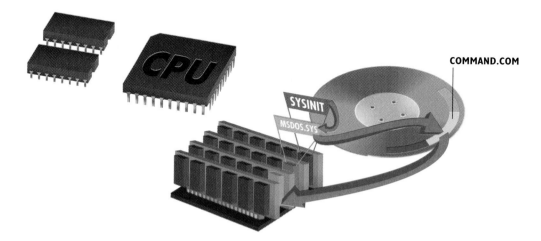

COMMAND.COM

6 SYSINIT tells MSDOS.SYS to load the file COMMAND.COM. This operating system file consists of three parts. One is a further extension to the input/output functions. This part is loaded in memory with the BIOS and becomes a part of the operating system.

7 The second part of COMMAND.COM contains the internal DOS commands such as DIR, COPY, and TYPE. It is loaded at the high end of conventional RAM, where it can be overwritten by applications programs if they need the memory.

ECHO OFF
prompt GP
SET TEMP=C:\Temp
PATH=C:\;C:\DOS

AUTOEXEC.BAT

8 The third part of COMMAND.COM is used only once and then discarded. This part searches the root directory for a file named AUTOEXEC.BAT. This file is created by the computer's user and contains a series of DOS batch file commands and/or the names of programs that the user wants to run each time the computer is turned on. The PC is now fully booted and ready to be used.

CHAPTER

3

How Plug and Play Works

UNTIL recently, when you bought a new expansion card for your computer, it was a nightmare trying to ensure that it got along peacefully with the other components already in your system. Problems arose because each component needs to communicate with the processor and other peripherals, and there are only a few channels for that communication. These channels are usually referred to as *system resources*. One resource is an *interrupt*. Another system resource is a direct line to memory called a DMA (direct memory access).

As its name suggests, an interrupt makes the processor interrupt whatever it's doing to take a look at the request a component is making for the processor's time. If two devices both use the same interrupt, the processor can't tell which device is asking for its attention. If two devices use the same DMA, one device will overwrite data the other has already stored in memory. When anything like this happens, it's called a *conflict*, and it's not a pretty sight.

In the dark ages of PCs—the decade of the eighties and half the nineties—there were two solutions to avoiding conflicts. One way was to be so anal-retentive that you had a complete record of every resource used by every device in your PC. Of course, no one had such records. So most people resolved conflicts by plugging in a new expansion card or drive, seeing if everything worked, and when it didn't—as is often the case the first time—folks pulled out the new device, and started over. That involved changing some nearly microscopic switches to change the resources the device used, plugging the device back in, rebooting, seeing if everything worked, and so on until finally you stumbled upon a combination that appeared to work.

There had to be a better way. And there is, now. Most PC companies, including the influential Microsoft and Intel, agreed to a system called, optimistically, Plug and Play. In theory, if every device in your PC conforms to the Plug and Play standard, the PC's BIOS (basic input/output system), various system software, and the devices themselves work together to automatically make sure no two of them compete for the same resources. Not every component uses Plug and Play, however. Look for it when buying components.

Before Plug and Play, if you wanted to add a piece of hardware to your system, you had to turn it off before installing the component. But Plug and Play lets you change devices on the fly without turning off the system—a process called *hot swapping*. It's most likely to crop up on notebooks or other PCs that use PCMCIA cards (PC cards).

The catch is that your PC, its BIOS, the peripherals, and your operating system all have to support Plug and Play. With the *laissez-faire* attitude many PC and component makers take toward standards, Plug and Play is not perfect. Windows 95 supplies many Plug and Play software drivers that other companies can use, but there's no way to make component manufacturers conform to the Plug and Play standard. Still, it's a big step toward hassle-free upgrading.

Plug and Play

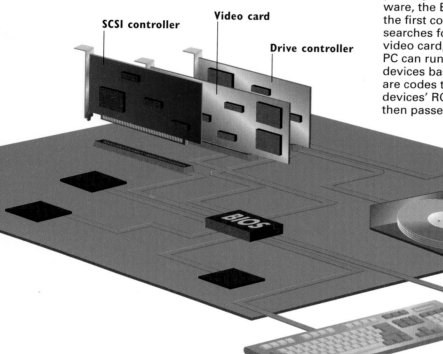

1 When you turn on a Plug and Play system, the primary arbitrator between software and hardware, the BIOS (basic input/output system) is the first component to take charge. The BIOS searches for all the devices it needs—such as a video card, keyboard, and floppy drive—so the PC can run properly. The BIOS identifies these devices based on their unique identifiers, which are codes that are burned permanently into the devices' ROM, or read-only memory. The BIOS then passes control to the operating system.

SCSI controller

Video card

Drive controller

2 The operating system executes special drivers called enumerators—programs that act as the interface between the operating system and the different devices. There are *bus enumerators*, enumerators for a special type of bus called *SCSI* (small computer system interface), *port enumerators*, and more. The operating system asks each enumerator to identify which devices the enumerator is going to control and what resources it needs.

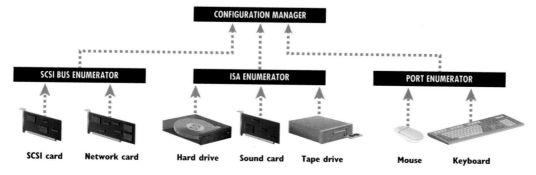

CONFIGURATION MANAGER

SCSI BUS ENUMERATOR

ISA ENUMERATOR

PORT ENUMERATOR

SCSI card   Network card   Hard drive   Sound card   Tape drive   Mouse   Keyboard

The operating system takes the information from the enumerators and stores it in a *hardware tree*, which is a database stored in RAM. The operating system then examines the hardware tree for *resource arbitration*. In other words, after storing the information in a database, the operating system decides what resources—interrupts (IRQs), for example—to allocate to each device. The system then tells the enumerators what resources it allocated to their respective devices. The enumerators save the resource allocation information in the peripherals' microscopic *programmable registers*, which are sort of digital scratchpads located in memory chips.

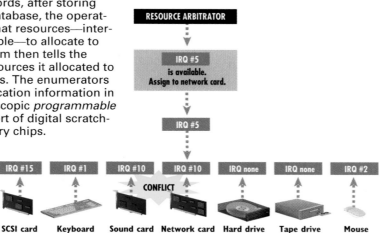

4 Finally, the operating system searches for the appropriate *device driver* for each device. A device driver is a small piece of add-on code for the operating system that tells the operating system the facts about a piece of hardware the system needs to communicate with it. If the system doesn't find a device driver it needs, it prompts you to install it. The system then loads all necessary device drivers, and tells each driver which resources its device is using. The device drivers initialize their respective devices, and the system finishes booting.

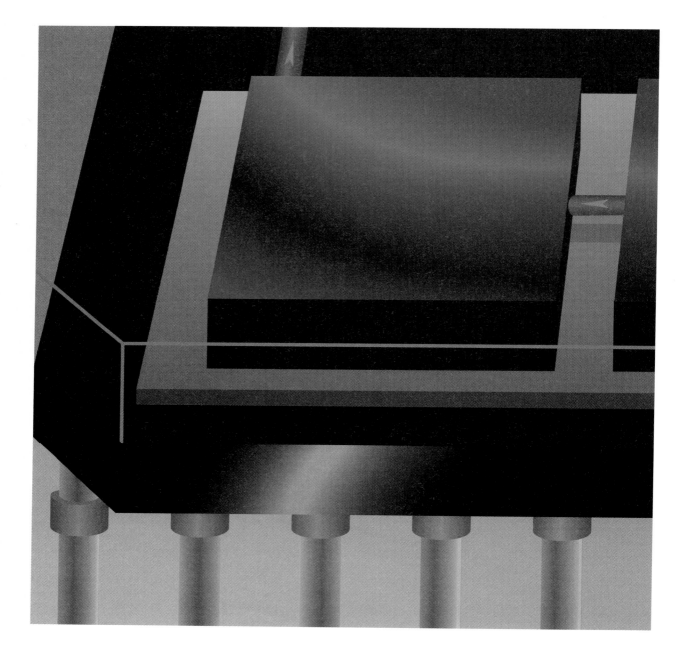

P A R T

MICROCHIPS

THE first computers used components called vacuum tubes. If you're not at least old enough to be part of the baby boom generation, you may never have seen more than one type of vacuum tube. They are no longer used in any electronic device, except for the gigantic vacuum tubes in your PC monitor and your TV screen.

Vacuum tubes functioned as electronic switches. When current flowed through one part of the tube, it made another component so hot that electrons boiled off and were attracted to a part of the tube that had a positive charge. A partial vacuum was needed inside the tube so that the electrons would encounter little resistance from molecules in air. When the electrons were flowing, the switch was on. When they weren't flowing, the switch was off.

Essentially a computer is just a collection of On/Off switches, which at first doesn't seem very useful. But imagine a large array of light bulbs—say, ten rows that each have 50 light bulbs in them. Each bulb is connected to a light switch. If you turn on the right combination of light bulbs, you can put your name in lights.

Computers are very similar to that bank of lights, with one important difference: A computer can sense which light bulbs are on and use that information to turn on other switches. If the pattern of On switches spells *Tom*, then the computer could be programmed to associate the *Tom* pattern with instructions to turn on another group of switches to spell *boy*. If the pattern spells *Mary*, the computer could turn on a different group of switches to spell *girl*. The two-pronged concept of On and Off maps perfectly with the binary number system, which uses only 0 and 1 to represent all numbers. By manipulating a roomful of vacuum tubes, early computer engineers could perform binary mathematical calculations, and by assigning alphanumeric characters to certain numbers, they could manipulate text.

The problem with those first computers, however, was that the intense heat generated by the hundreds of vacuum tubes made them notoriously unreliable. The heat caused many components to deteriorate and consumed enormous amounts of power. But for vacuum tubes to be on, the tubes didn't really need to generate the immense flow of electrons that they created. A small flow would do quite nicely, but vacuum tubes were big. They worked on a human scale in which each part could be seen with the naked eye. They were simply too crude to produce more subtle flows of electrons. Transistors changed the way computers could be built.

A transistor is essentially a vacuum tube built, not on a human scale, but on a microscopic scale. Because it is small, it requires less power to generate a flow of electrons. Because it uses less power, a transistor generates less heat, making computers more dependable. And the microscopic scale of transistors means that a computer that once took up an entire room now fits neatly on your lap.

All microchips, whether they're microprocessors, a memory chip, or a special-purpose integrated circuit, are basically vast collections of transistors arranged in different patterns so that they accomplish different tasks. Currently, the number of transistors that can be created on a single chip is about 3.1 million. The physical limitation is caused by how narrowly manufacturers can focus the beams of light used to etch away transistor components made of light-sensitive materials. Chip makers are experimenting with X rays instead of ordinary light because X rays are much narrower. Someday, transistors may be taken to their logical extreme—the molecular level, in which the presence or absence of just one electron signals an On or Off state.

CHAPTER

4

How a Transistor Works

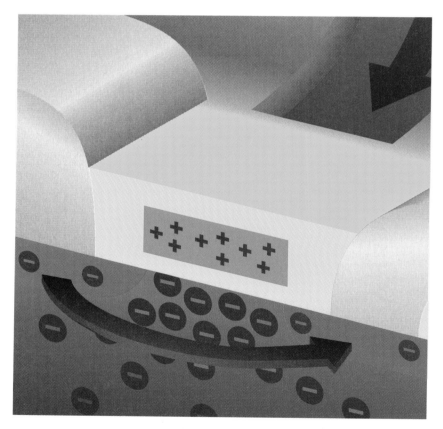

THE transistor is the basic building block from which all microchips are built. The transistor can only create binary information: a 1 if current passes through or a 0 if current doesn't. From these 1s and 0s, called *bits*, a computer can create any number, provided it has enough transistors grouped together to hold the 1s and 0s required.

Binary notation starts off simply enough:

Decimal Number	Binary Number	Decimal Number	Binary Number
0	0	6	110
1	1	7	111
2	10	8	1000
3	11	9	1001
4	100	10	1010
5	101		

Personal computers such as those based on the Intel 8088 and 80286 microprocessors are 16-bit PCs. That means they can work directly with binary numbers of up to 16 places or bits. That translates to the decimal number 65,536. If an operation requires numbers larger than that, the PC must first break those numbers into smaller components, perform the operation on each of the components, and then recombine the results into a single answer. More powerful PCs, such as those based on the Intel 80386, 80486, and Pentium, are 32-bit computers, which means they can manipulate binary numbers up to 32 bits wide—the equivalent in decimal notation of 4,294,967,296. The ability to work with 32 bits at a time helps make these PCs so much faster.

Transistors are not used simply to record and manipulate numbers. The bits can just as easily stand for true (1) or not true (0), which allows computers to deal with Boolean logic. Combinations of transistors in various configurations are called *logic gates*, which are combined into arrays called *half adders*, which in turn are combined into *full adders*. More than 260 transistors are needed to create a full adder that can handle mathematical operations for 16-bit numbers.

In addition, transistors make it possible for a small amount of electrical current to control a second, much stronger current—just as the small amount of energy needed to throw a wall switch can control the more powerful energy surging through the wires to a light.

Transistor

1 A small positive electrical charge is sent down one aluminum lead that runs into the transistor. The positive charge is transferred to a layer of conductive polysilicon buried in the middle of nonconductive silicon dioxide.

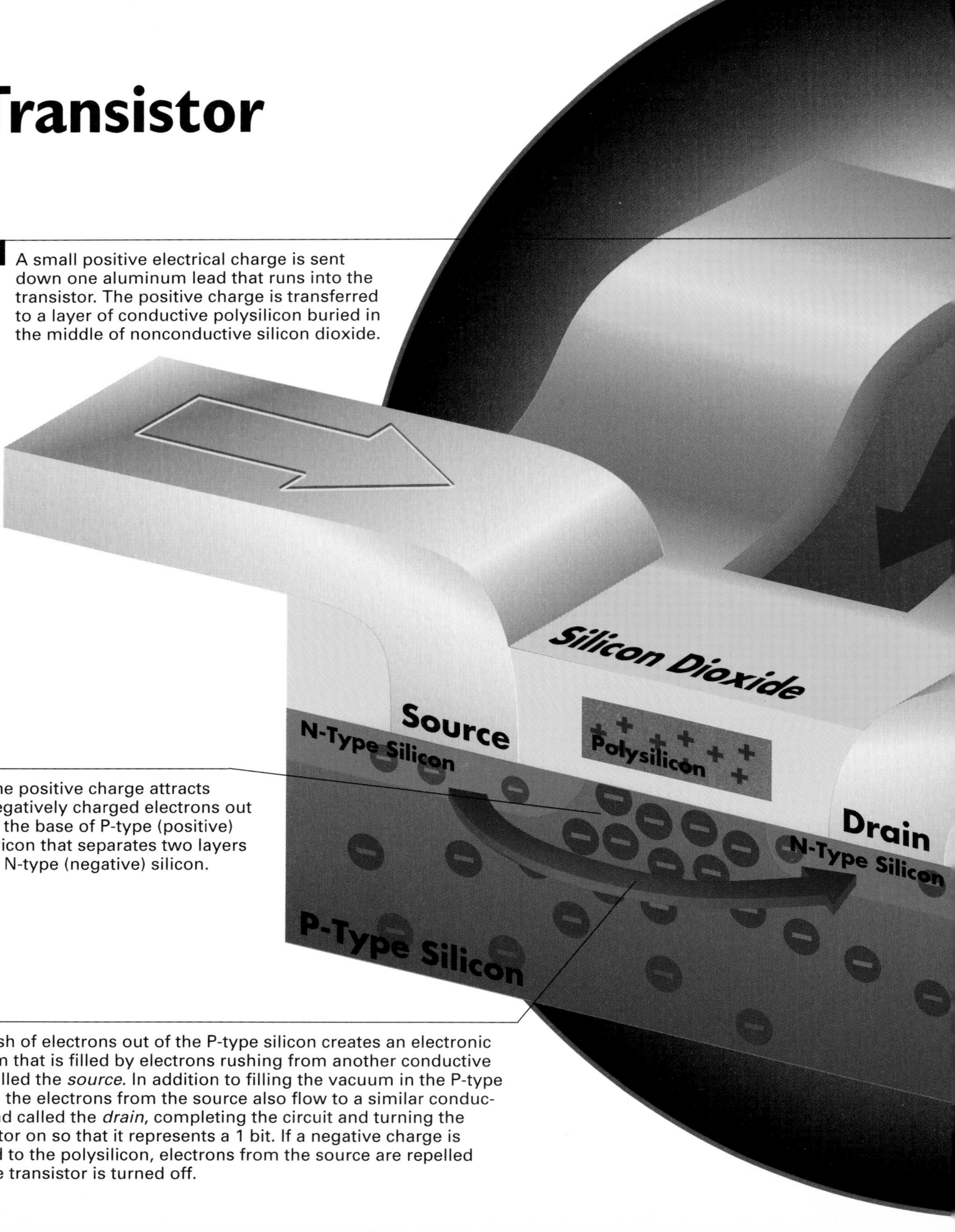

Silicon Dioxide

Source
N-Type Silicon

Polysilicon

Drain
N-Type Silicon

2 The positive charge attracts negatively charged electrons out of the base of P-type (positive) silicon that separates two layers of N-type (negative) silicon.

P-Type Silicon

3 The rush of electrons out of the P-type silicon creates an electronic vacuum that is filled by electrons rushing from another conductive lead called the *source*. In addition to filling the vacuum in the P-type silicon, the electrons from the source also flow to a similar conductive lead called the *drain*, completing the circuit and turning the transistor on so that it represents a 1 bit. If a negative charge is applied to the polysilicon, electrons from the source are repelled and the transistor is turned off.

NOTE Thousands of transistors are combined on a single slice of silicon. The slice is embedded in a piece of plastic and attached to metal leads that expand to a size that makes it possible to connect the chip to other parts of a computer circuit. The leads carry signals into the chip and send signals from the chip to other computer components.

C H A P T E R

5

How RAM Works

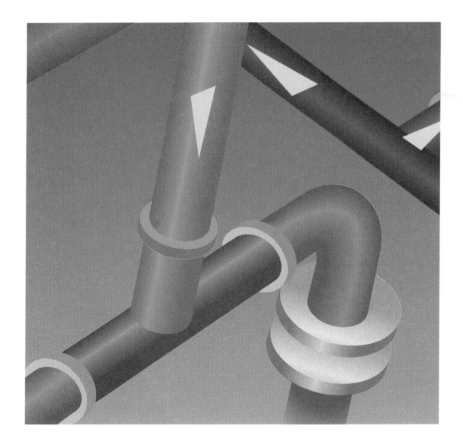

RANDOM

RANDOM Access Memory (RAM) chips are to your computer what a blank canvas is to an artist. Before a PC can do anything useful, it must move programs from disk to RAM. The data contained in documents, spreadsheets, graphics, databases, or any type of file must also be stored in RAM, if only momentarily, before the software can use the processor to manipulate that data.

Regardless of what kind of data a personal computer is using and regardless of how complex that data may appear to us, to the PC that data exists only as 0s and 1s. Binary numbers are the native tongue of computers because even the biggest, most powerful computer essentially is no more than a collection of switches: An open switch represents a 0; a closed switch represents a 1. This is sometimes referred to as a computer's machine language. From this simplest of all numeric systems, your computer can construct representations of millions of numbers, any word in any language, and hundreds of thousands of colors and shapes.

Because humans are not nearly as fluent at binary notation as computers are, all those binary numbers appear on screen in some understandable notation—usually the alphabet or decimal numbers. For example, when you type an uppercase *A*, the operating system and software use a convention known as *ASCII,* in which certain numbers represent certain letters. A computer is essentially a number manipulator, which is why it's easier at the machine level for computers to deal with binary numbers. But it's easier for programmers and other humans to use decimal numbers. The capital *A* is the decimal number 65; *B* is 66; *C* is 67; and so on. Still, in the heart of a computer, the numbers are stored in their binary equivalents.

It is these binary notations that fill your disks and the PC's memory. But when you first turn on your computer, its RAM is a blank slate. The memory is filled with 0s and 1s that are read from disk or created by the work you do with the computer. When you turn off your PC, anything that's contained in RAM disappears. Some newer forms of RAM chips retain their electrical charges when a computer is turned off. But most memory chips work only if there is a source of electricity to constantly refresh the thousands or millions of individual electrical charges that make up the programs and data stored in RAM.

Writing Data to RAM

1 Software in combination with the operating system sends a burst of electricity along an *address line*, which is a microscopic strand of electrically conductive material etched onto a RAM chip. This burst identifies where to record data among the many address lines in a RAM chip.

2 At each memory location in a RAM chip where data can be stored, the electrical pulse turns on (closes) a transistor that's connected to a data line. A *transistor* is essentially a microscopic electrical switch.

3 While the transistors are turned on, the software sends bursts of electricity along selected data lines. Each burst represents a *bit*—either a 1 or a 0, in the native language of processors, and the ultimate unit of information that a computer manipulates.

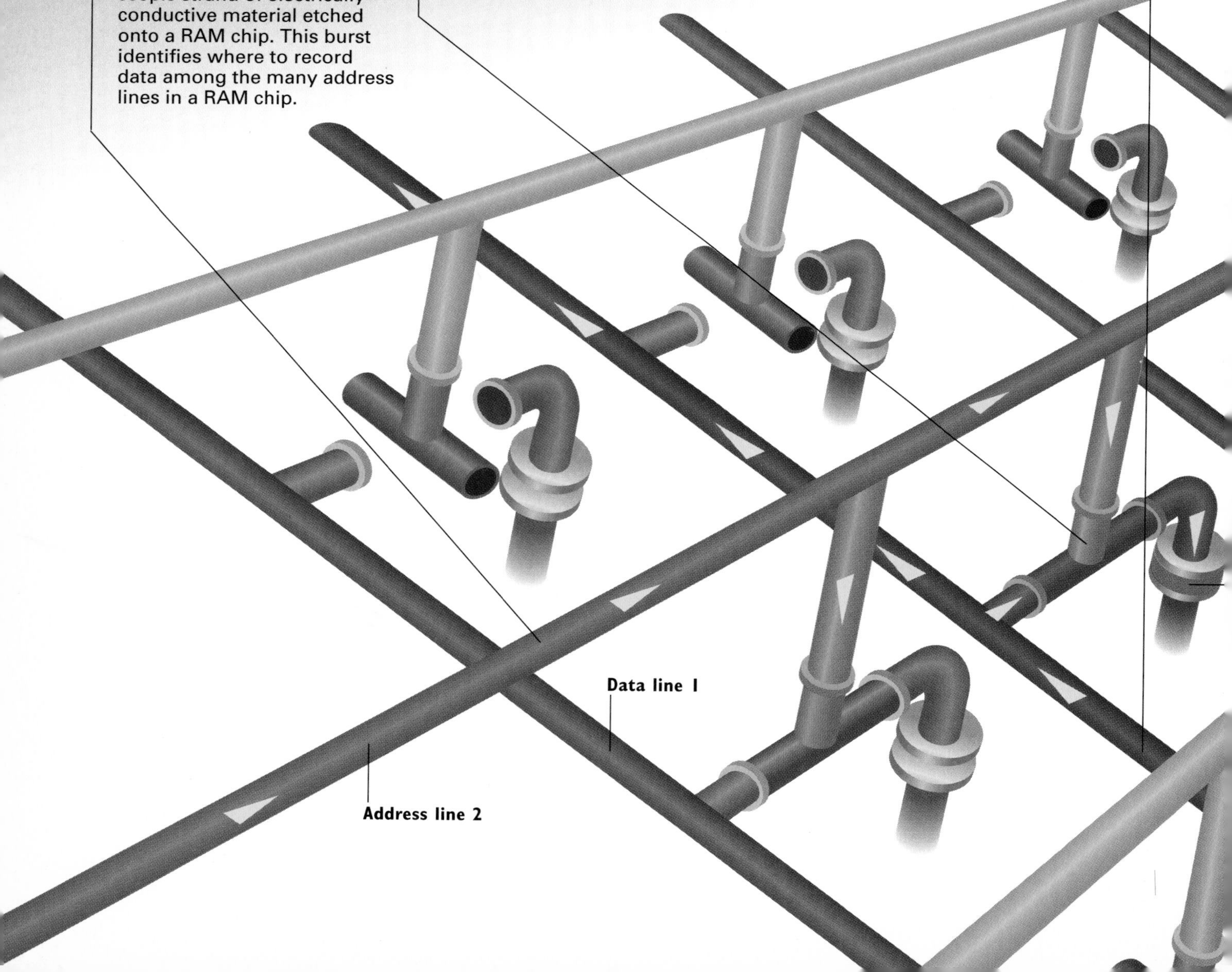

Data line 1

Address line 2

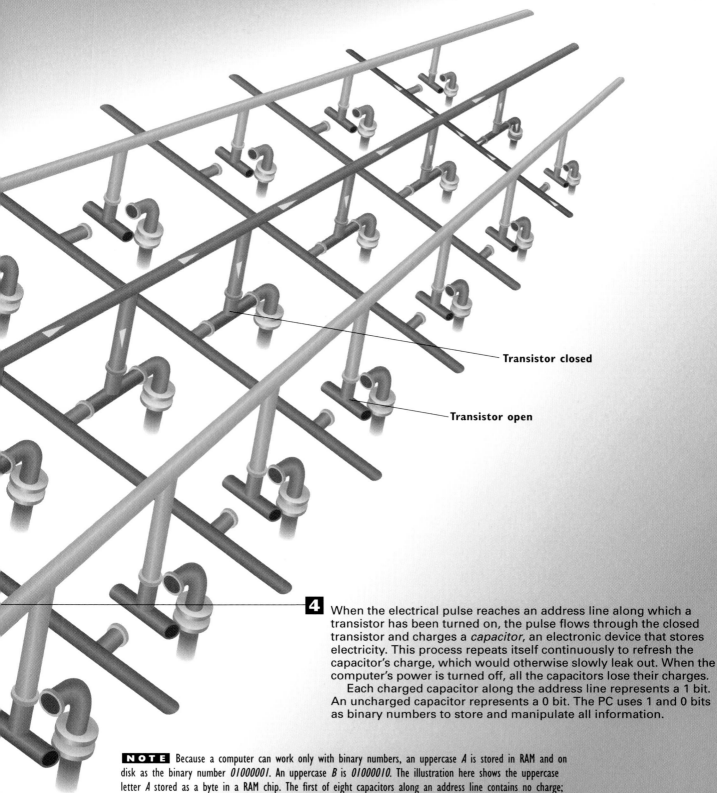

Transistor closed

Transistor open

4 When the electrical pulse reaches an address line along which a transistor has been turned on, the pulse flows through the closed transistor and charges a *capacitor*, an electronic device that stores electricity. This process repeats itself continuously to refresh the capacitor's charge, which would otherwise slowly leak out. When the computer's power is turned off, all the capacitors lose their charges.

Each charged capacitor along the address line represents a 1 bit. An uncharged capacitor represents a 0 bit. The PC uses 1 and 0 bits as binary numbers to store and manipulate all information.

NOTE Because a computer can work only with binary numbers, an uppercase *A* is stored in RAM and on disk as the binary number *01000001*. An uppercase *B* is *01000010*. The illustration here shows the uppercase letter *A* stored as a byte in a RAM chip. The first of eight capacitors along an address line contains no charge; the second capacitor is charged; the next five capacitors have no charge; and the eighth capacitor is charged.

Reading Data from RAM

2 Everywhere along the address line that there is a capacitor holding a charge, the capacitor will discharge through the circuit created by the closed transistors, sending electrical pulses along the data lines.

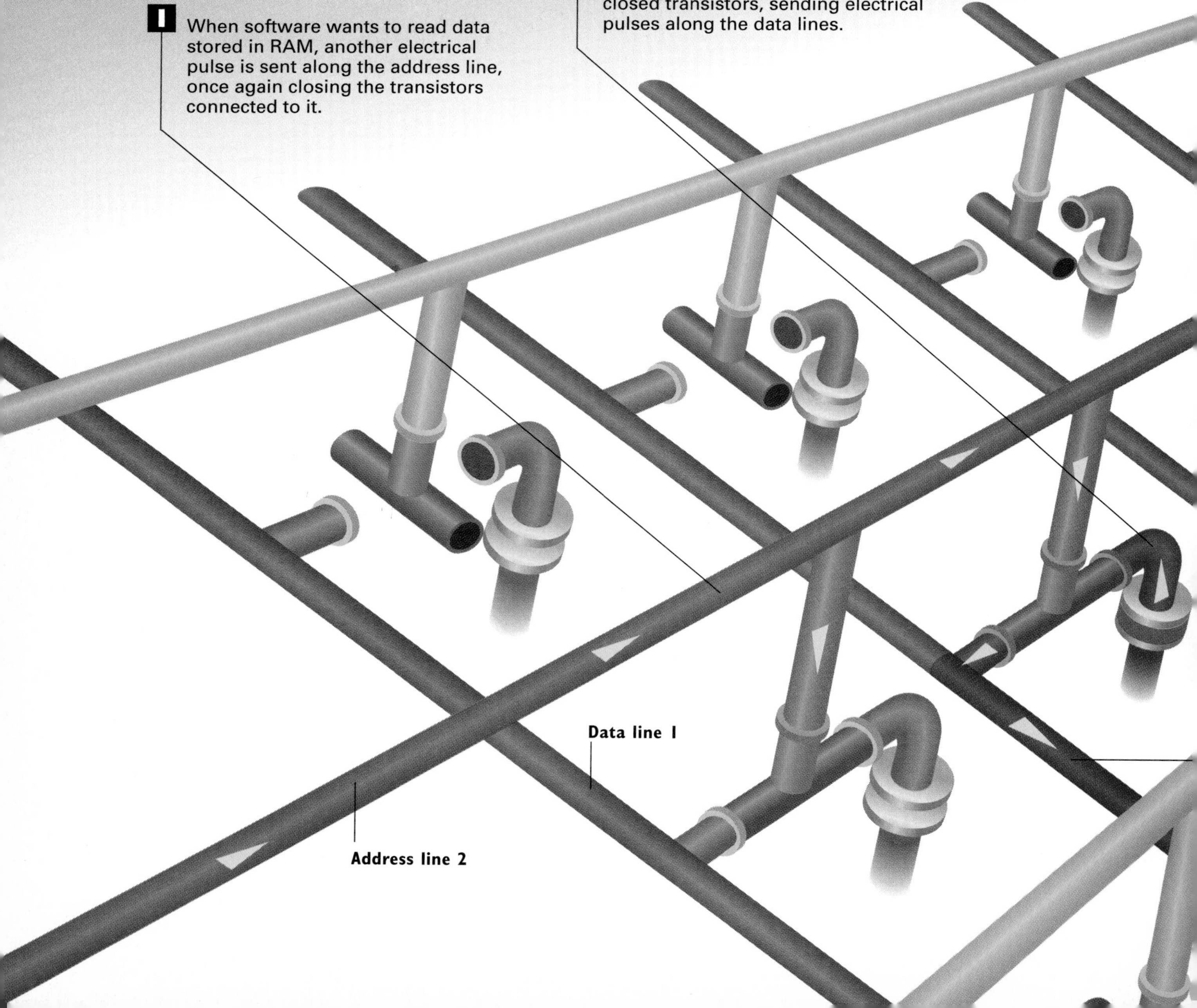

1 When software wants to read data stored in RAM, another electrical pulse is sent along the address line, once again closing the transistors connected to it.

Data line 1

Address line 2

3 The software recognizes which data lines the pulses come from, and interprets each pulse as a 1, and any line on which a pulse is not sent as a 0. The combination of 1s and 0s from eight data lines forms a single byte of data.

CHAPTER
6

How a Computer Performs Addition

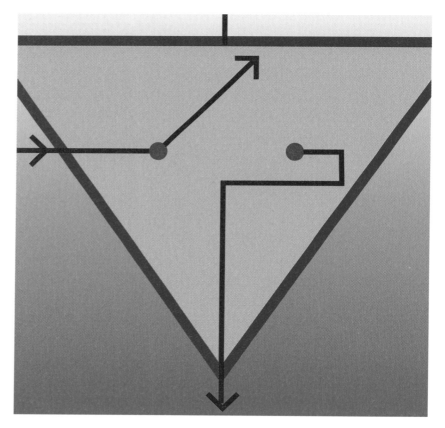

THE easiest way to visualize how computers work is to think of them as enormous collections of switches, which is really what they are—switches in the form of microscopic transistors etched into a slice of silicon. But for the moment, think of a computer as being a giant billboard made up of columns and rows of lights—thousands of them. Then imagine a control room behind that billboard in which there is a switch for each one of the light bulbs on the sign. By turning on the correct switches you can spell your name or draw a picture.

But suppose there are "master switches" that control dozens of other switches. Instead of having to flip each switch individually for every light bulb that goes into spelling your name, you can throw one switch that lights up a combination of lights to create a B, then another master switch that turns on all the lights for an O, then another switch to light up another B.

Now you're very close to understanding how a computer works. In fact, substitute a computer display for the billboard and substitute RAM—which is a collection of transistorized switches—for the control room, and a keyboard for the master switches, and you have a computer performing one of its most basic functions, displaying what you type on screen.

Of course, a computer has to do a lot more than display words to be helpful. But the off and on positions of the same switches used to control a display also can add numbers by representing the 0 and 1 in the binary number system. And once you can add numbers, you can perform any kind of math because multiplication is simply repeated addition, subtraction is adding a negative number, and division is repeated subtraction. And to a computer, everything—math, words, numbers, and software instructions—is numbers. This fact lets all those switches (transistors) do all types of data manipulation.

Actually, the first computers were more like our billboard in how they were used. They didn't have keyboards or displays. The first computer users did actually throw a series of switches in a specific order to represent both data and the instructions for handling that data. Instead of transistors, the early computers used vacuum tubes, which were bulky and generated an enormous amount of heat. To get the computer's answer, the people using it had to decipher what looked like a random display of lights. Even with the most underpowered PC you can buy today, you've still got it a lot better than the earliest computer pioneers.

How a Computer Performs Addition

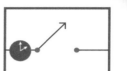 

1 All information—words and graphics as well as numbers—is stored in and manipulated by a PC in the form of binary numbers. In the binary numerical system there are only two digits—0 and 1. All numbers, words, and graphics are formed from different combinations of those two digits.

Decimal	Binary
0	0
1	1
2	10
3	11
4	100
5	101
6	110
7	111
8	1000
9	1001
10	1010

2 Transistor switches are used to manipulate binary numbers because there are two possible states of a switch, open (off) or closed (on), which nicely matches the two binary digits. An open transistor, through which no current is flowing, represents a 0. A closed transistor, which allows a pulse of electricity from the PC's clock to pass through, represents a 1. (The computer's clock regulates how fast the computer works. The faster a clock ticks or emits pulses, the faster the computer works. Clock speeds are measured in megahertz, or millions of ticks per second.) Current passing through one transistor can be used to control another transistor, in effect turning the switch on and off to change what the second transistor represents. Such an arrangement is called a *gate* because, like a fence gate, the transistor can be open or closed, allowing or stopping current flowing through it.

3 The simplest operation that can be performed with a transistor is called a *NOT logic gate*. It takes one input from the clock and one from another transistor. The NOT gate produces a single output—one that's always the opposite of the input from the other transistor. The NOT gate has only a single transistor. When current from another transistor representing a 1 is sent to a NOT gate, the gate's own transistor switch opens so that a pulse, or currents, from the clock can't flow through it, which makes the NOT gate's output 0. A 0 input closes the NOT gate's transistor so that the clock pulse passes through it to produce an output of 1.

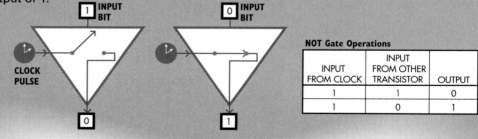

NOT Gate Operations

INPUT FROM CLOCK	INPUT FROM OTHER TRANSISTOR	OUTPUT
1	1	0
1	0	1

4 NOT gates strung together in different combinations create other logic gates, all of which have a line to receive pulses from the clock and two other input lines for pulses from other logic gates. The *OR gate* creates a 1 if either the first *or* the second input is a 1.

OR Gate

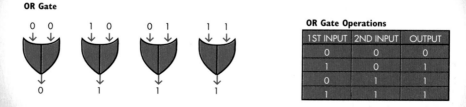

OR Gate Operations

1ST INPUT	2ND INPUT	OUTPUT
0	0	0
1	0	1
0	1	1
1	1	1

5 An *AND gate* outputs a 1 only if the first input *and* the second input are 1s.

AND Gate

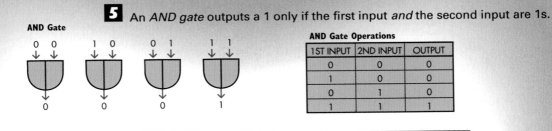

AND Gate Operations

1ST INPUT	2ND INPUT	OUTPUT
0	0	0
1	0	0
0	1	0
1	1	1

6 An *XOR* gate puts out a 0 if both the inputs are 0 or if both are 1. It generates a 1 only if one of the inputs is one and the other is a zero.

XOR Gate

XOR Gate Operations

1ST INPUT	2ND INPUT	OUTPUT
0	0	0
1	0	1
0	1	1
1	1	0

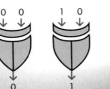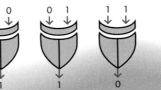

7 With different combinations of logic gates, a computer performs the math that is the foundation of all its operations. This is accomplished with gate designs called *half-adders* and *full-adders*. A half-adder consists of an XOR gate and an AND gate, both of which receive the same input representing one-digit binary numbers. A full-adder consists of half-adders and other switches.

8 A combination of a half-adder and a full-adder handles larger binary numbers and can generate results that involve carrying over numbers. To add the decimal numbers 2 and 3 (10 and 11 in the binary system), first the half-adder processes the digits on the right side through both XOR and AND gates.

9 The result of the XOR operation—1—becomes the rightmost digit of the result.

10 The result of the half-adder's AND operation—0—is sent to XOR and AND gates in the full adder. The full-adder also processes the lefthand digits from 11 and 10, sending both of them to another XOR gate and another AND gate.

11 The results from XORing and ANDing the lefthand digits are processed with the results from the half-adder. One of the new results is passed through an OR gate.

12 The result of all the calculation is 101 in binary, which is 5 in decimal. For larger numbers, more full-adders are used—one for each digit in the binary numbers. An 80386 or later processor uses 32 full-adders.

CHAPTER

7

How a Microprocessor Works

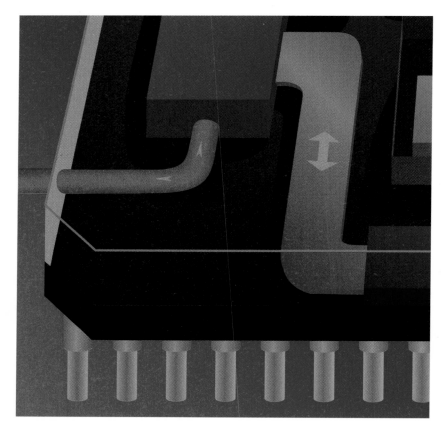

THE microprocessor that makes up your personal computer's central processing unit, or CPU, is its brains, messenger, ringmaster, and boss. All the other components—RAM, disk drives, the monitor—exist only to bridge the gap between you and the processor. They take your data and turn it over to the processor to manipulate; then they display the results. The CPU isn't the only microprocessor in many PCs today. Coprocessors on Windows accelerator video cards and sound cards juggle display and sound data to relieve the CPU of part of its burden. And some special processors, such as the one inside your keyboard that handles the signals coming from a stream of key presses, perform specialized tasks designed to get data into or out of the CPU.

The current standard for high-performance processors is Intel's Pentium chip. On a chip of silicon roughly an inch square, the Pentium holds 3.1 million transistors, or tiny electronic switches. All the operations of the Pentium are performed by signals turning on or off different combinations of those switches. In computers, transistors are used to represent 0s and 1s, the two numbers that make up the binary number system. These 0s and 1s are commonly known as *bits*. Various groupings of these transistors make up the subcomponents within the Pentium.

Most of the components of the Pentium are designed to get data in and out of the chip quickly and to make sure that the parts of the Pentium that do the actual data manipulation never have to go into idle because they're waiting on more data or instructions. These components have to handle the flow of data and instructions through the processor, interpret the instructions so they can be executed by the processor, and send the results back to the PC's memory. The ideal is that the processor is executing an instruction for each tick of the computer's clock, which regulates how fast the system works.

The Pentium has several improvements over its predecessor, Intel's 80486 processor, that help ensure data and code move through the Pentium as fast as possible. One of the most important changes is in the arithmetic logic unit (ALU). Just think of the ALU as sort of a brains within the brains. The ALU handles all the data juggling that involves integers, or whole numbers such as 1, 23, 610, 234, or −123. The Pentium is the first Intel processor to have two ALUs so that it can crunch two sets of numbers at the same time. Like the 486, the Pentium has a separate calculation unit that's optimized for handling floating-point numbers, or numbers with decimal fractions, such as 1.2, 35.8942, .317 or −93.2.

Another significant difference over the 486 is that the Pentium can take in data 64 bits at a time, compared to the 32-bit data path of the 486. Where the 486 has one storage area called a cache that holds 8 kilobytes at a time, the Pentium has two 8K caches. One cache is for data and the other is for coded instructions; both are designed to make sure the ALU is constantly supplied with the data and instructions it needs to do its job. In many operations, the Pentium runs software twice as fast as the 486. But the full potential of the Pentium is not achieved unless the software is created especially to use the unique abilities of the Pentium processor.

Microprocessor

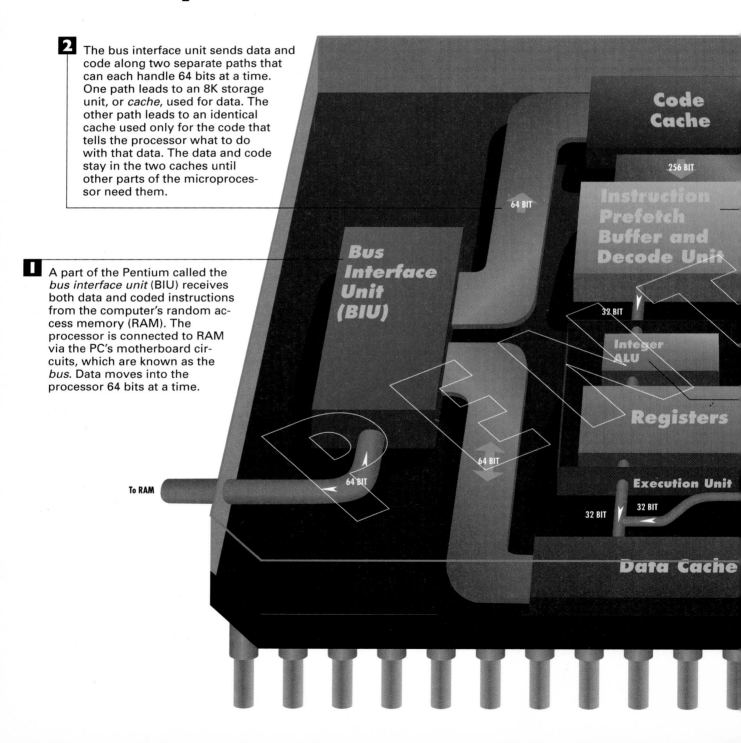

2 The bus interface unit sends data and code along two separate paths that can each handle 64 bits at a time. One path leads to an 8K storage unit, or *cache*, used for data. The other path leads to an identical cache used only for the code that tells the processor what to do with that data. The data and code stay in the two caches until other parts of the microprocessor need them.

1 A part of the Pentium called the *bus interface unit* (BIU) receives both data and coded instructions from the computer's random access memory (RAM). The processor is connected to RAM via the PC's motherboard circuits, which are known as the *bus*. Data moves into the processor 64 bits at a time.

Code Cache

256 BIT

Instruction Prefetch Buffer and Decode Unit

64 BIT

Bus Interface Unit (BIU)

32 BIT

Integer ALU

Registers

64 BIT

Execution Unit

To RAM

64 BIT

32 BIT   32 BIT

Data Cache

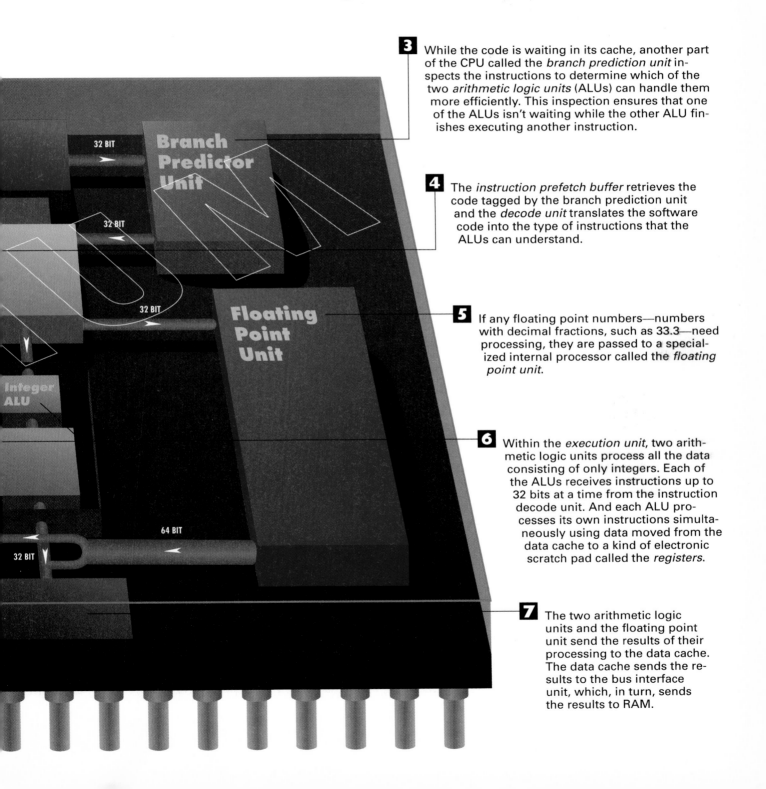

3 While the code is waiting in its cache, another part of the CPU called the *branch prediction unit* inspects the instructions to determine which of the two *arithmetic logic units* (ALUs) can handle them more efficiently. This inspection ensures that one of the ALUs isn't waiting while the other ALU finishes executing another instruction.

4 The *instruction prefetch buffer* retrieves the code tagged by the branch prediction unit and the *decode unit* translates the software code into the type of instructions that the ALUs can understand.

5 If any floating point numbers—numbers with decimal fractions, such as 33.3—need processing, they are passed to a specialized internal processor called the *floating point unit*.

6 Within the *execution unit*, two arithmetic logic units process all the data consisting of only integers. Each of the ALUs receives instructions up to 32 bits at a time from the instruction decode unit. And each ALU processes its own instructions simultaneously using data moved from the data cache to a kind of electronic scratch pad called the *registers*.

7 The two arithmetic logic units and the floating point unit send the results of their processing to the data cache. The data cache sends the results to the bus interface unit, which, in turn, sends the results to RAM.

Branch
Predictor
Unit

Floating
Point
Unit

Integer
ALU

32 BIT

32 BIT

32 BIT

64 BIT

32 BIT

CHAPTER

8

How CISC and RISC Processors Work

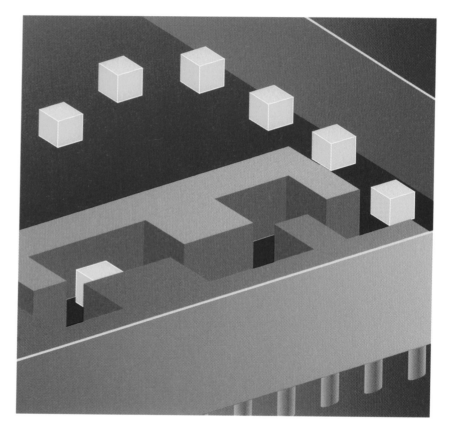

THROUGH most of the history of personal computers, the predominant form of microprocessor has been from Intel Corp. The first processor in a IBM PC was Intel's 8088. The generations of Intel processors that followed it were in the '86 family—the 8086, 80286, 80386 and 80486. All were more elaborate versions of the original 8088, but improved on its performance by one of two ways—operating faster or handling more data simultaneously. The 8088, for example, operated at 4.7MHz—or 4.7 million frequency waves a second—and some 80486 chips go as fast as 100MHz. The 8088 could handle 8 bits of data at a time, and the 80486 handles 32 bits internally.

But despite the changes, the Intel processors through the 80486 were based on a design philosophy called CISC, for *complex instruction set computing*. CISC uses commands that incorporate many small instructions to carry out a single operation. It is a broadsword in how it chops and slices data and code. An alternative design, by comparison, works more like a scalpel, cutting up smaller, more delicate pieces of data and code. The scalpel is called *reduced instruction set computing* (RISC). RISC designs are found in newer processors such as the DEC Alpha, IBM's RISC 6000, the Power PC processor, and, to an extent, the Intel Pentium processors.

RISC is a less complicated design that uses several simpler instructions to execute a comparable operation in less time than a single CISC processor executes a large, complicated command. RISC chips can be physically smaller than CISC chips. And because they use fewer transistors, they're generally cheaper to produce and are less prone to overheating.

There have been many predications that the future of processors is in RISC design, and that's probably correct. But there has not been a wholesale movement to RISC because of two reasons. The most important is to maintain compatibility with the vast number of software applications that have been written to work with Intel's earlier CISC processors.

The second reason is that you don't really receive the full benefit of RISC architecture unless you're using an operating system and programs that have been written and *compiled* specifically to take advantage of RISC operations. It's a classic chicken-and-egg situation. Some computer manufacturers are offering RISC processors as a way of projecting themselves to the leading edge of technology. They run old CISC programs only by emulating a CISC processor, which negates the RISC advantages. So most PC makers have stayed with the design that's where the money is. At the same time, software creators are reluctant to convert their programs to RISC-compiled versions when there aren't that many people who have RISC-based PCs.

Most likely, processors will continue along the safer evolutionary path Intel is following. Eventually, we'll wind up using RISC architecture, but most computer users won't really know when their PCs cross the dividing line between the two designs.

CISC and RISC Processors

Complex Instruction Set Computing (CISC)

1 Built into a CISC microprocessor's read-only memory is a large set of commands containing several subcommands that must be carried out to complete a single operation, such as multiplying two numbers or moving a string of text to another location in memory. Whenever the operating system or application software requires the processor to perform a task, the program sends the processor the name of the command along with any other information it needs, such as the locations in RAM of the two numbers to be multiplied.

2 Because CISC commands are not all the same size, the microprocessor examines the command to determine how many bytes of processing room the command requires and then sets aside that much internal memory. There are also several different ways the commands can be loaded and stored, and the processor must determine the correct way to load and store each of the commands. Both of these preliminary tasks slow down execution time.

3 The processor sends the command requested by the software to a *decode unit*, which translates the complex command into *microcode*, a series of smaller instructions that are executed by the *nanoprocessor*, which is like a processor within the processor.

5 The nanoprocessor executes each of the microcode instructions through circuitry that is complex because the instructions may need to pass through several different steps before they are all fully executed. Moving through the complex circuits requires more time. CISC processors typically require between four and ten clock cycles to perform a single instruction. In an extreme case an 80386 may take as many as 43 clock cycles to perform a single mathematical operation.

4 Because one instruction may depend on the results of another instruction, the instructions are performed one at a time. All other instructions stack up until the current instruction is completed.

Reduced Instruction Set Computing (RISC)

2 All RISC commands are the same size, and there is only one way in which they can be loaded and stored. In addition, since each command is already a form of microcode, RISC processors don't require the extra step of passing instructions they receive through a decode unit to translate complex commands into simpler microcode. As a result of these differences, RISC commands are loaded for execution far more quickly than CISC commands.

1 Command functions built into a RISC processor consist of several small, discrete instructions that perform only a single job. Application software, which must be recompiled especially for a RISC processor, performs the task of telling the processor which combination of its smaller commands to execute in order to complete a larger operation.

3 During the compilation of software specifically for a RISC chip, the compiler determines which commands will not depend on the results of other commands. Because these commands don't have to wait on other commands, the processor can simultaneously execute as many as 10 commands in parallel.

4 Because the RISC processor is dealing with simpler commands, its circuitry also can be kept simple. RISC commands pass through fewer transistors on shorter circuits, so the commands execute more quickly. The result is that RISC processors usually require only one CPU clock cycle per instruction. The number of cycles required to complete a full operation is dependent on the number of small commands that make up that operation. But, for a comparable operation, the time required to interpret and execute RISC instructions is far less than the time needed to load and decode a complex CISC command and then execute each of its components.

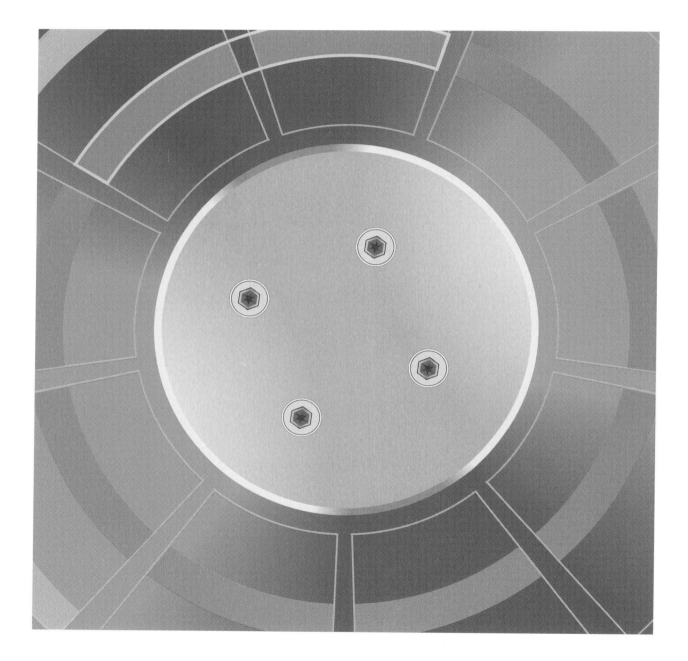

P A R T

DATA
STORAGE

As intelligent and swift as a computer's memory may be, RAM has one fatal flaw. It is a will-o'-the wisp. With a few exceptions, all memory chips lose the information stored in them once you turn off the computer. All the work you've put into figuring out next year's budget, creating account billings, or writing the great American sitcom will vanish if the electricity constantly stoking the RAM chips' transistors falters for even a fraction of a second.

Fortunately, there are several ways to provide permanent storage for a computer's programs and the work they generate—storage that stays intact even when the power is turned off. The most common form of permanent storage is magnetic disks—both the floppy and hard variety. Magnetic storage is also used in the form of tape drives—a method of permanent storage that's been around almost as long as the first computers. Gaining popularity are new devices that use lasers to store or retrieve data. And recently, computer manufacturers have made strides toward creating nonvolatile memory chips that, unlike their more common RAM chip cousins, don't lose their contents when you turn off your PC because they have their own built-in power supplies. All of these methods of permanently storing data have their advantages and disadvantages.

Floppy disks are universal, portable, and inexpensive but lack both large capacity and speed. Hard disks are probably the best all-around storage medium. They store and retrieve data quickly, have the capacity to save several volumes of data, and are inexpensive on a cost-per-megabyte basis. But hard disks are generally not portable. Tape drives provide virtually endless off-line storage at low cost, but they are too slow to use as anything other than a backup medium.

Some of the newer forms of storage serve PC users who need to store enormous quantities of data. CD-ROM drives covered, in Chapter 24, pack up to 650 megabytes of data on a disc identical to the laser compact discs that play music, and CD-ROM discs are cheap to produce. But they are read-only devices, which means that you can only use the data that was stored on them when they were created; you can't erase or change the data on a CD-ROM. Magneto-optical drives and floptical drives, like CD-ROMs, use lasers to read data. However, they have the advantage that their data can be modified. They are fast, portable, and have generous storage capacities, but only recently has their cost dropped low enough to make them common.

Two types of memory chips retain their information once they are no longer refreshed with electricity. EPROMs (for Erasable Programmable Read-Only Memory) are found in nearly every personal computer. They are the chips that supply boot-up information to the

PC. But they are slow, and their data can be changed only by exposing them first to ultraviolet light. Flash RAM chips, which combine the writability and much of the speed of conventional RAM chips with the ability to retain data when the main power source is turned off, promise to be in common use in the future and may turn out to be the ideal permanent storage medium. But for now, they are too expensive to completely replace hard disks. You'll find them most often in PC cards (Chapter 23).

Despite the different technologies behind these methods of storage, they all have in common a similar notation for recording data and a similar system for filing that information so that it can be found again. Permanent data storage is similar in concept to paper filing systems. Paper files may be handwritten or typed, but they are all in the same language. And just as paper files thrown willy-nilly into file cabinets would be impossible to retrieve easily and quickly, electronic files to be retrieved must be stored, too, in an orderly and sensible system and in a common language.

In this part of the book, we'll look at how various forms of permanent storage solve the task of saving data so that it can easily be found again, and how different storage devices write and retrieve that data.

CHAPTER

9

How Disk Storage Works

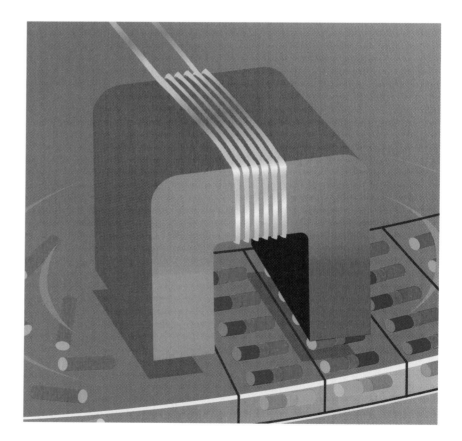

DISKS are the most common form of permanent data storage. Their capacities may range from a few hundred kilobytes to several gigabytes, but they all have some elements in common. For one, the way that a drive's mechanism creates the 1s and 0s that make up the binary language of computers may differ, but the goal is to alter microscopically small areas of the disk surface so some of the areas represent 0s and others represent 1s. The disk has no other characters with which it records a great novel or this week's grocery list.

Another common element is the scheme that determines how the data on the disk is organized. The computer's operating system, which on most personal computers is MS-DOS, determines the scheme. The operating system controls so many of a PC's operations that many PC users forget that *DOS* stands for *Disk Operating System* and that, originally, its primary function was to control disk drives.

Before any information can be stored on a magnetic disk, the disk must first be formatted. Formatting creates a road map that allows the drive to store and find data in an orderly manner. The road map consists of magnetic codes that are embedded in the magnetic film on the surface of the disk. The codes divide the surfaces of the disk into *sectors* (pie slices) and *tracks* (concentric circles). These divisions organize the disk so that data can be recorded in a logical manner and accessed quickly by the read/write heads that move back and forth over the disk as it spins. The number of sectors and tracks that fit on a disk determines the disk capacity.

After a disk is formatted, writing or reading even the simplest file is a complicated process. This process involves your software, operating system, the PC's BIOS (Basic Input/Output System), *drivers* that tell the operating system how to use add-on hardware, such as a SCSI drive or a tape drive, and the mechanism of the disk drive itself.

Writing and Reading Bits on a Disk

1 Before any data is written to a disk, iron particles are scattered in a random pattern within a magnetic film that coats the surface of the disk. The film is similar to the surface of audio and video tapes. To organize the particles into data, electricity pulses through a coil of wire wrapped around an iron core in the drive mechanism's read/write head; the head is suspended over the disk's surface. The electricity turns the core into an electromagnet that can magnetize the molecules in the coating, much like a child uses a magnet to play with iron filings.

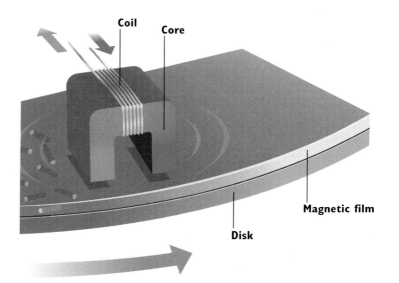

Coil Core

Magnetic film

Disk

2 The coil induces a magnetic field in the core as it passes over the disk. The field, in turn, magnetizes the iron molecules in the disk coating so their positive poles point toward the negative pole of the read/write head, and their negative poles point to the head's positive pole. The positive and negative poles are represented here as red and blue, respectively.

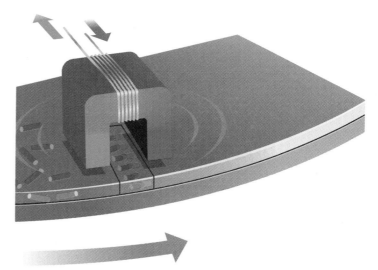

3 After the head creates one magnetic band on the revolving disk, a second band is created next to it. Together, the two bands represent the smallest discrete element of data that a computer can handle—a bit. If the bit is to represent a binary 1, after creating the first band, the current in the coil reverses so that the magnetic poles of the core are swapped and the molecules in the second band are magnetized in the opposite direction. If the bit is a binary 0, the molecules in both bands are aligned in the same direction.

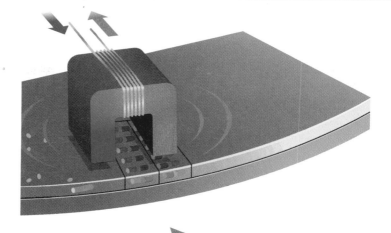

4 When a second bit is stored, the polarity of its first band is always the opposite of the band preceding it to indicate that it's beginning a new bit. Even the slowest drive takes only a fraction of a second to create each band. The stored bits in the illustration below represent the binary number 1011, which is 11 in decimal numbers.

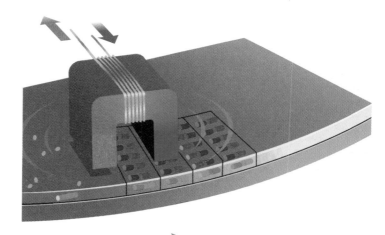

5 To read the data, no current is sent to the read/write head as it passes over the disk. Instead, the magnetic reverse of the writing process happens. The banks of polarized molecules in the disk's coating are themselves tiny magnets that create a magnetic field through which the read/write head passes. The movement of the head through the magnetic field generates an electrical current that travels in one direction or the other through the wires leading from the head. The direction the current flows depends on the polarities of the bands. By sensing the directions in which the current is moving, the computer can tell if the read/write head is passing over a 1 or a 0.

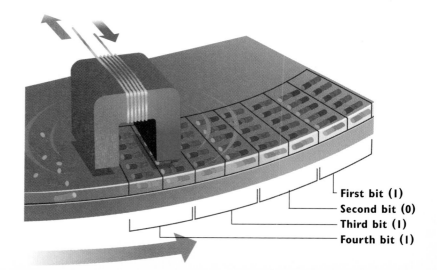

First bit (1)
Second bit (0)
Third bit (1)
Fourth bit (1)

Formatting a Disk

1 The first task a magnetic drive must do is to format any disk that is used with it. It does this by writing onto the surface of the disk a pattern of 1s and 0s—like magnetic signposts. The pattern divides the disk radially into sectors and concentric circles. As the read/write head moves back and forth over the spinning disks, it reads these magnetic signposts to determine where it is in relation to the data on the disk's surface.

2 The combination of two or more sectors on a single track makes up a *cluster* or *block*. The number of bytes in a cluster may vary according to the version of DOS used to format the disk and the disk's size. A cluster is the minimum unit DOS uses to store information. Even if a file has a size of only 1 byte, an entire 256–byte cluster may be used to hold the file. The number of sectors and tracks and, therefore, the number of clusters that a drive can create on a disk's surface determine the capacity of the disk.

3 The drive creates a special file located in the disk's sector 0. (In the computer world, numbering often begins with 0 instead of 1.) This file is the file allocation table, or FAT. The FAT is where DOS stores the information about the disk's directory structure and what clusters are used to store which files. In newer versions of DOS, an identical copy of the FAT is kept in another location in case the data in the first FAT becomes corrupted. Ordinarily, you will never see the contents of either FAT.

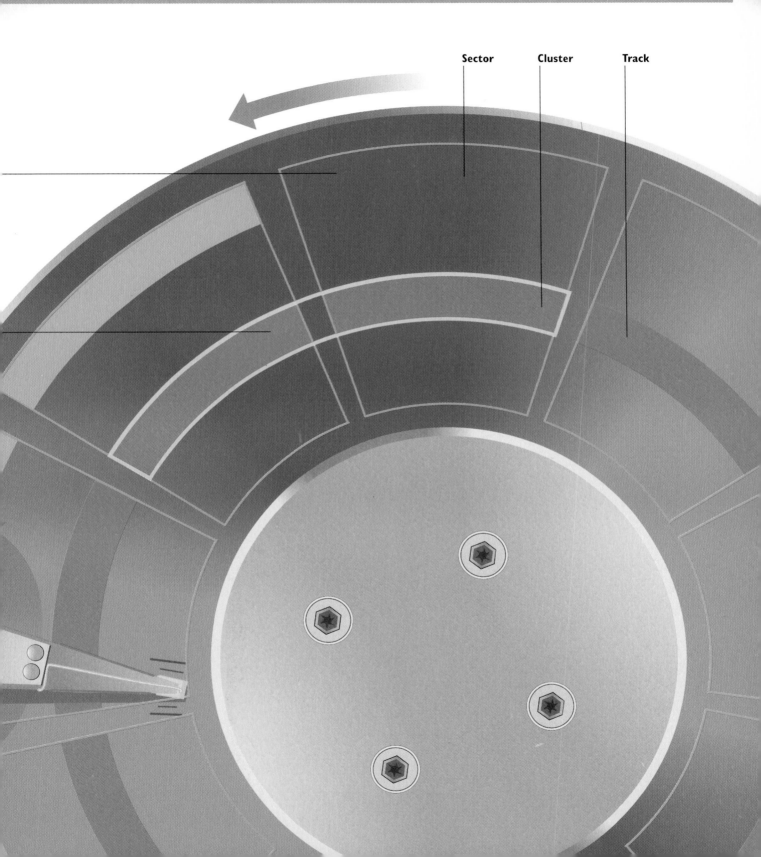

Sector   Cluster   Track

CHAPTER

10

How a Floppy Drive Works

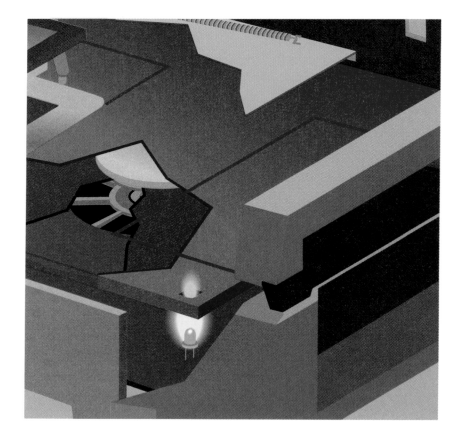

AMID
superfast, superbig hard drives, magneto-optical drives, CD-ROM drives, and all the other newest high-tech marvels, it's hard to get excited about the common floppy drive. It's slow and doesn't store very much compared to any other type of drive.

But for all its deficiencies, the floppy drive is an underappreciated wonder. An entire bookful of information can be contained on a disk that you can slip into your pocket or a briefcase. Floppy drives are ubiquitous, making them a sure and convenient way to get data from one PC to another. No communication lines, networks, or infrared links are needed; just pull the floppy out of one machine and slip it into another.

With his NeXT computer, Steve Jobs tried to eliminate the floppy entirely and promote the magneto-optical drive as the ideal method of distributing commercial software. The idea had a note of technological idealism to it, but no one thought very highly of it. For all its commoner heritage, the floppy is dependable and respectable. It will be with us in some form for a long time to come.

Although smaller, faster, and more capacious floppy drives are now standard components of all new computers, it took years for them to supplant the old 5.25-inch floppy drive. It was the 78-rpm phonograph record of the computer world. Long after smaller records that played more music with greater fidelity were available, phonograph companies continued to produce turntables with 78-rpm settings just because many music lovers had so much invested in 78s. You'll still see 5.25-inch drives today, but they're quickly becoming antiques.

With capacities today ranging from 700 kilobytes to 2.88 megabytes, 3.5-inch disks hold more data than their bigger cousins. Their protective cases mean that we can be downright careless about how we handle them, and they are so cheap that their cost is not a factor. They are now the standard for distributing new software and for storing portable data.

3.5-inch Floppy Drive

1 When a 3.5-inch floppy disk is inserted into the drive, it presses against a system of levers. One lever opens the shutter to expose the *cookie*—the mylar disk coated on either side with a magnetic material that can record data.

7 When the heads are in the correct position, electrical impulses create a magnetic field in one of the heads to write data to either the top or bottom surface of the disk. When the heads are reading data, they react to magnetic fields generated by the metallic particles on the disk.

6 A stepper motor—which can turn a specific amount in either direction according to signals from the circuit board—moves a second shaft that has a spiral groove cut into it. An arm attached to the read/write heads rests inside the shaft's groove. As the shaft turns, the arm moves back and forth, positioning the read/write heads over the disk.

5 A motor located beneath the disk spins a shaft that engages a notch on the hub of the disk, causing the disk to spin.

NOTE Despite its different size and casing, the 5.25-inch floppy disk is simply a bigger, slower, less complicated version of the 3.5-inch disk. It has no door to open, but the notch on its side is checked for write protection, and the read/write heads of the drive work identically to those of the smaller drive.

2 Other levers and gears move two read/write heads until they almost touch the cookie on either side. The heads, which are tiny electromagnets, use magnetic pulses to change the polarity of metallic particles embedded in the disk's coating.

3 The drive's circuit board receives signals, including data and instructions for writing that data to disk, from the floppy drive's controller board. The circuit board translates the instructions into signals that control the movement of the disk and the read/write heads.

4 If the signals include instructions to write data to the disk, the circuit board first checks to make sure that no light is visible through a small, closable window in one corner of the disk's housing. But if the window is open and a beam from a light-emitting diode can be detected by a photo-diode on the opposite side of the disk, the drive knows the disk is write-protected and refuses to record new data.

CHAPTER

11

How a Hard Drive Works

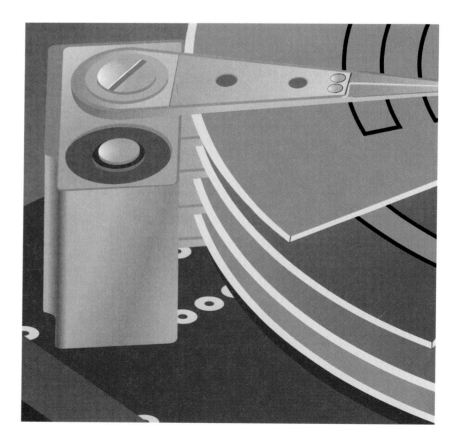

A hard drive is the workaholic of a PC system. The platters on which data is stored spin at a breakneck speed as long as the computer is turned on (unless they periodically power down to conserve electricity). Each access of the hard drive to read or write a file causes the read/write heads to burst into a furious flurry of movement—which must be performed with microscopic precision. So exacting are the tolerances in a hard drive—the gaps between the heads and the platters aren't big enough to admit a human hair—that it's a wonder the drive can perform its work at all without constant disasters. Instead, it keeps on plugging away as the repository of perhaps years of work—with surprisingly few failures.

The capacity, form, and performance of hard drives have changed dramatically since the introduction of the first IBM XT with a hard drive in the early 1980s. Back then, a capacity of 10 megabytes was considered generous. The hard drive was 3 to 4 inches thick and filled a 5.25-inch drive bay. An access time of 87 milliseconds was warp speed compared to the access times of floppy drives. A decade later, hard drives that hold 500 megabytes in a size smaller than that of a 3.5-inch floppy drive and with access speeds of 14 milliseconds are inexpensive and commonplace. Some hard drives pack dozens of megabytes on removable disks no larger than a matchbox. In the future, the size of drives will continue to decrease at the same time that their capacities increase.

One thing about hard drives will probably stay the same. Unlike other PC components that obey the commands of software without complaint, the hard drive chatters and groans as it goes about its job. Those noises are reminders that the hard drive is one of the few components of a personal computer that is mechanical as well as electronic. The drive's mechanical components, in more ways than one, make it where the action is.

Hard-Disk Drive

3 A spindle connected to an electrical motor spins as many as eight magnetically coated platters at several thousand rotations per minute. The number of platters and the composition of the magnetic material coating them determine the capacity of the drive. Today's platters, typically, are coated with an alloy about 3 millionths of an inch thick.

2 On the bottom of the drive, a printed circuit board, also known as a logic board, receives commands from the drive's controller, which in turn is controlled by the operating system. The logic board translates those commands into voltage fluctuations that force the head actuator to move the read/write heads across the platters' surfaces. The board also makes sure that the spindle turning the platters is revolving at a constant speed, and the board tells the drive heads when to read and when to write to the disk. On an IDE (Integrated Drive Electronics) disk, the disk controller is part of the logic board.

1 A sealed metal housing protects the internal components from dust particles that could block the narrow gap between the read/write heads and the platters and cause the drive to crash by plowing a furrow in a platter's magnetic coating.

4 A head actuator pushes and pulls the gang of read/write head arms across the surfaces of the platters with critical precision. It aligns the heads with the tracks that lie in concentric circles on the surface of the platters.

5 Read/write heads, attached to the ends of the moving arms, slide in unison across the surfaces of the hard drive's spinning platters. The heads write the data coming from the disk controller to the platters by aligning magnetic particles on the platters' surfaces; the heads read data by detecting the polarities of particles that have already been aligned.

6 When you or your software tell the operating system to read or write a file, the operating system orders the hard-disk controller to move the read/write heads to the drive's file allocation table, or FAT in DOS (VFAT in Windows 95). The operating system reads the FAT to determine in which clusters on the disk a preexisting file begins, or which portions of the disk are available to hold a new file.

7 A single file may be strewn among hundreds of separate clusters scattered across several platters. The operating system stores a file beginning in the first clusters it finds listed as free in the FAT. The FAT keeps a chained record of the clusters used by a file, each link in the chain leading to the next cluster containing more of the file.

Once the data from the FAT has passed through the drive's electronics and hard-disk controller back to the operating system, the operating system instructs the drive to skip its read/write heads across the surface of the platters, reading or writing clusters on the platters spinning past the heads.

After the operating system writes a new file to the disk, it sends the read/write heads back to the FAT, where it records a list of all the file's clusters.

CHAPTER

CHAPTER

12

How Magneto-Optical and Floptical Drives Work

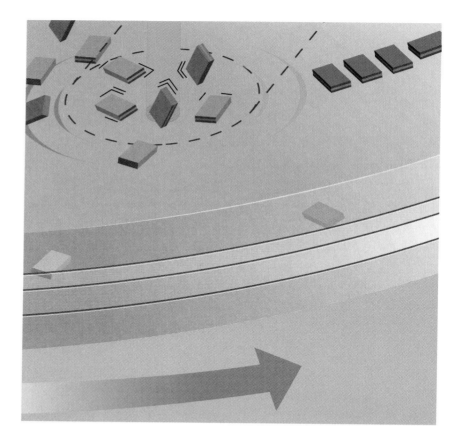

THE magnetic signals used by conventional floppy drives and hard disks save data in strips that are microscopically small. But get down on their level, and the magnetic signals are grossly crude. The area affected by the electromagnets in read/write heads, microscopically speaking, is a wide, wandering river. You could put a lot more data on the same size disk if you could just restrict the data to narrow, tightly packed channels. You can—if you combine magnetism with the precision of a laser.

A beam of light produced by a laser can be narrowed to a much smaller area than that affected by a magnetic read/write head. But harnessing lasers alone to write as well as read data isn't easy or cheap. Instead, a combination of magnetic heads with the precision of a laser beam creates a drive that puts a lot of data into a very small—and portable—package.

The first attempts to combine lasers and storage resulted in something called a *WORM*. Standing for Write Once, Read Many, a WORM could, indeed, pack hundreds of megabytes of data onto a single, removable disk. The problem with WORM is that once data was written to a disk, it could not be changed—or even deleted. An elaborate file-tracking scheme made it possible for a new version of a file to be written to the disk while hiding the original version. The scheme was okay as a work-around but still not an ideal solution. Theoretically, it was possible to fill a 500MB WORM disk with a single 1K file. Today, WORM drives are most useful in situations in which you want to keep an unalterable audit trail of transactions.

Two other types of drives—magneto-optical (MO) and floptical—approach the challenge of using lasers from different angles, but both wind up in the same neighborhood: More writable data storage. A magneto-optical disk is about 5¼ inches in diameter, similar to larger floppy disks. It contains up to 500MB, and magneto-optical drives that can hold twice that much information are being developed. A floptical disk is the same size as a 3½-inch floppy. It holds up to 20 megabytes.

Although MO drives and flopticals use technologies that are different from each other and from that in CD-ROMs, they are similar in that all use lasers to pack data so tightly that you can save dozens to hundreds of megabytes of information on a single disk—a disk you can move from one machine to another. But CD-ROM drives that you can write to are expensive and temperamental. MO drives and flopticals are reasonably priced alternatives to CD-ROM and tape drives for backup, offline storage, and transfer of large files from one PC to another.

Magneto-Optical and Floptical Drives

A Magneto-Optical Drive

1 The electromagnetic read/write head of the drive generates a magnetic field that covers a relatively large area on the magneto-optical drive's disk. But the crystalline metal alloy that covers the surface of the disk is too stable to be affected by the magnetic field alone.

2 A thin, precise laser beam is focused on the surface of the disk. The energy in the beam heats up a tiny spot in the alloy to a critical temperature known as its *Curie point*. At this point, the heat loosens the metallic crystals in the alloy enough that they can be moved by the write head's magnetic field, which aligns the crystals in one direction to represent a 0 bit and a different direction to represent a 1 bit.

3 To read data from a magneto-optical disk, a weaker laser beam is focused along the tracks of data that had been created with the help of the more intense laser.

4 The crystals in the alloy *polarize* the light from the laser. Polarization allows only light vibrating in a certain direction to pass through the crystals. The alignment of crystals in 0 bits polarizes the light in one direction, and the crystals in 1 bits polarize light in a different direction.

5 The polarized light is reflected from the aluminum layer of the disk to a *photo diode*, which senses the direction in which the light is polarized and translates that information into a stream of 0s and 1s.

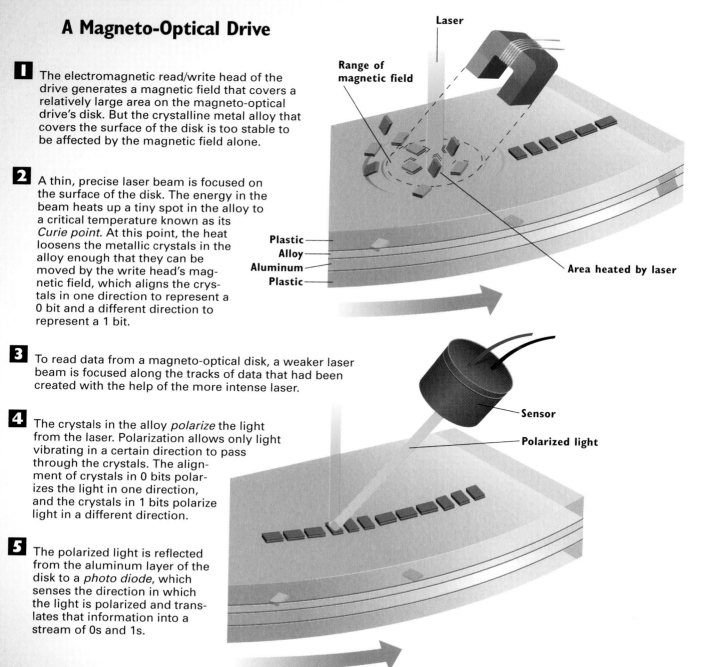

Laser

Range of magnetic field

Plastic
Alloy
Aluminum
Plastic

Area heated by laser

Sensor

Polarized light

A Floptical Drive

Tracks on floptical disk

Tracks on ordinary floppy

1 A floptical disk is created with a series of small, precise concentric tracks stamped in its barium-ferrite surface coating. The tracks, which is where data is written, are thinner and more numerous than those created by ordinary disk formatting. On conventional floppies the operating system formats the disk by recording magnetic markers on the surface of the disk to create a roadmap of tracks and sectors. The markers are used to find areas where files exist or where new files can be written. But this method of formatting has wide tolerances for error to allow for the imprecision with which the drive head reads those markers. Those wide margins limit how much can be stored on a regular floppy.

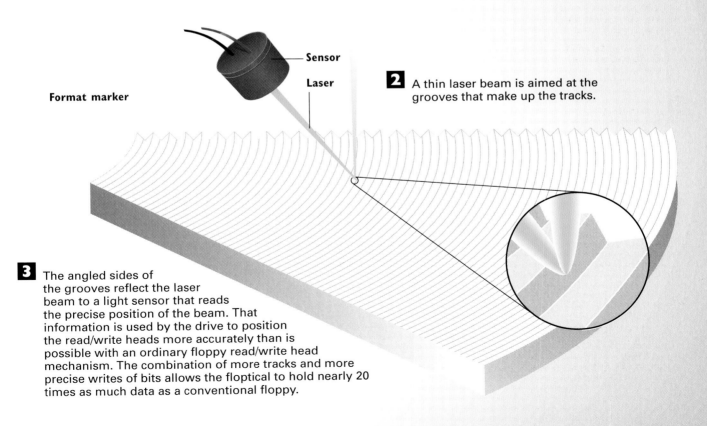

Sensor

Laser

Format marker

2 A thin laser beam is aimed at the grooves that make up the tracks.

3 The angled sides of the grooves reflect the laser beam to a light sensor that reads the precise position of the beam. That information is used by the drive to position the read/write heads more accurately than is possible with an ordinary floppy read/write head mechanism. The combination of more tracks and more precise writes of bits allows the floptical to hold nearly 20 times as much data as a conventional floppy.

CHAPTER

13

How a Tape Backup Drive Works

BACKING up your hard disk to a tape drive used to be like one of your mother's warnings when you were a child: Take an umbrella with you on cloudy days and always wear a raincoat. Sure, Mom was right once in a while—rain would come down and you would get wet, but it wasn't all that terrible. So what if your hard disk's file allocation table got scrambled and you lost half your files. A few years ago, as long as you'd copied a few essential data files to floppies, recreating a couple of megabytes of programs from their original distribution disks wasn't that much trouble.

Today, however, the implications of a "little" hard-disk disaster have mushroomed. You're more often talking about hard drives that contain not just a few megs of files, but hundreds. A single Windows program may include 30 megabytes of files. And with a complex environment such as Windows, no program exists alone. Many Windows programs you install modify at least one of the .INI files of Windows. Plus, how many tweaks have you made to your system—from arcane parameters to a memory manager's device-driver line in CONFIG.SYS to the Windows color scheme you spent hours perfecting—tweaks you could never hope to remember?

At the same time that it becomes more critical than ever to back up hard drives, disk sizes up to 500 megabytes make the idea of backing up to floppy disks even more abhorrent. Enter the new breed of less expensive, more capacious tape backup drives. Prices well under $500 make them affordable even for home systems. And the ability to copy a gigabyte or more to a single tape makes them simple to use for even the biggest hard drives.

Here are the workings inside two of the most popular types of tape backups: quarter-inch cartridge (QIC) and digital audio tape (DAT).

Quarter-inch Cartridge (QIC) Tape Backup Drive

1 When you use the software for a quarter-inch cartridge drive to issue a backup command, the program reads your hard disk's file allocation table to locate the files you've told it to back up. The software writes the directory information to a 32K buffer in your PC's RAM. It then copies the files into the same buffer. Each file is prefaced with header information that identifies the file and its location on the hard drive's directory tree.

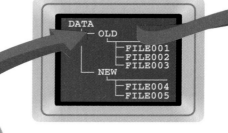

6 As either end of the tape approaches the drive head, holes punched in the tape signal the drive to reverse the direction of the tape and to shift the active area of the recording head up or down to the next track and then continue recording. When all the data has been written to the tape, the backup software updates the tape's directory with the track and segment locations of the files that it's backed up.

5 The format of a QIC tape typically contains 20 to 32 parallel tracks. When the tape reaches either end of a spool, its movement reverses and the flow of data loops back in a spiral fashion to the next outside track. Each track is divided into blocks of 512 or 1,024 bytes, and segments typically contain 32 blocks. Of the blocks in a segment, eight contain error-correction codes. In addition, at the end of each block, the drive computes a *cyclic redundancy check* (CRC) for further error correction and appends it to the block. Most backup software reserves space for a directory of backed-up files at the beginning of track 0 or in a separate directory track.

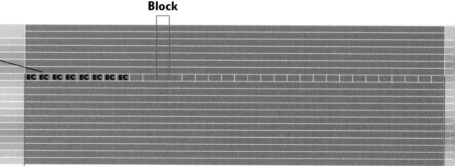

Block

Segment

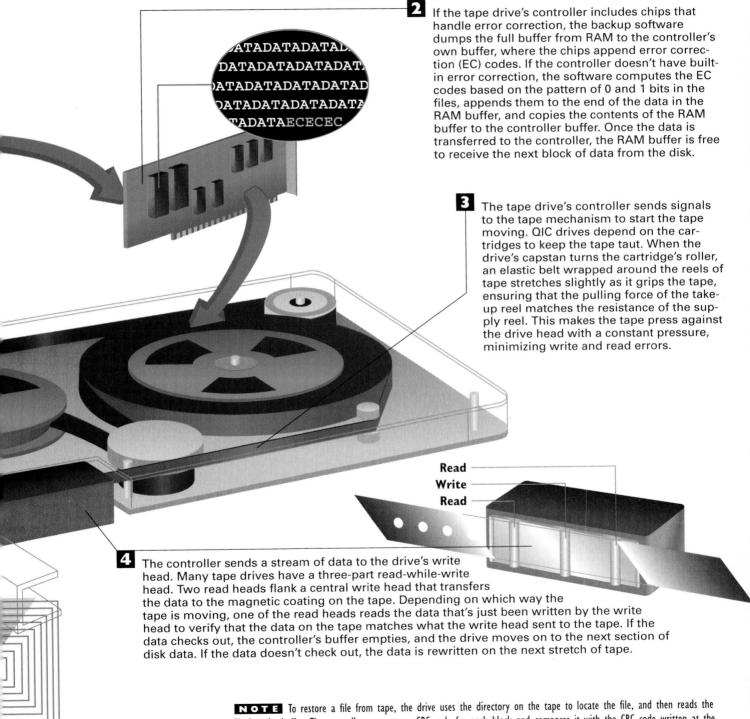

2 If the tape drive's controller includes chips that handle error correction, the backup software dumps the full buffer from RAM to the controller's own buffer, where the chips append error correction (EC) codes. If the controller doesn't have built-in error correction, the software computes the EC codes based on the pattern of 0 and 1 bits in the files, appends them to the end of the data in the RAM buffer, and copies the contents of the RAM buffer to the controller buffer. Once the data is transferred to the controller, the RAM buffer is free to receive the next block of data from the disk.

3 The tape drive's controller sends signals to the tape mechanism to start the tape moving. QIC drives depend on the cartridges to keep the tape taut. When the drive's capstan turns the cartridge's roller, an elastic belt wrapped around the reels of tape stretches slightly as it grips the tape, ensuring that the pulling force of the take-up reel matches the resistance of the supply reel. This makes the tape press against the drive head with a constant pressure, minimizing write and read errors.

Read
Write
Read

4 The controller sends a stream of data to the drive's write head. Many tape drives have a three-part read-while-write head. Two read heads flank a central write head that transfers the data to the magnetic coating on the tape. Depending on which way the tape is moving, one of the read heads reads the data that's just been written by the write head to verify that the data on the tape matches what the write head sent to the tape. If the data checks out, the controller's buffer empties, and the drive moves on to the next section of disk data. If the data doesn't check out, the data is rewritten on the next stretch of tape.

NOTE To restore a file from tape, the drive uses the directory on the tape to locate the file, and then reads the file into its buffer. The controller computes a CRC code for each block and compares it with the CRC code written at the end of the block. If there's a discrepancy, error-correction routines usually can fix the data using the EC codes appended to each data block. As the tape drive's buffer fills up, data is written to the hard disk in the appropriate directory.

Digital Audio-Tape (DAT) Backup Drive

1 When you issue a backup command from your software, the program checks your hard disk's file allocation table to find the files to back up. Then it copies the data, file by file, into the digital audio tape drive's buffer, which usually has room for 512K or 1MB of data. Like a QIC tape drive, the DAT drive performs an algorithm on the data to create error-correction code that it adds to the data in the buffer.

3 During the time that write head A is in contact with the tape, it writes about 128K of data and error-correction codes from the drive's buffer to a track on the tape. Because the cylinder is tilted, the head encounters one edge of the tape at the beginning of the write head and moves diagonally across the tape until it reaches the other side. This results in a narrow diagonal track about eight times longer than the width of the tape.

4 Read head A reads back and verifies the data in track A, bit by bit, against the data still in the buffer. If the data on the tape checks out, it's flushed from the buffer, and more data is read from the hard disk. If the data in track A contains errors, the data will be rewritten on the next pass.

Write head A

Read head A

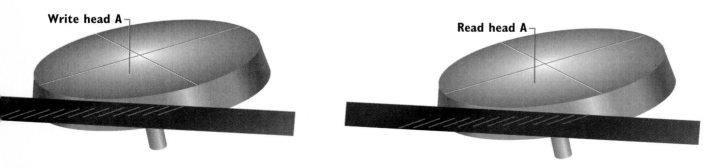

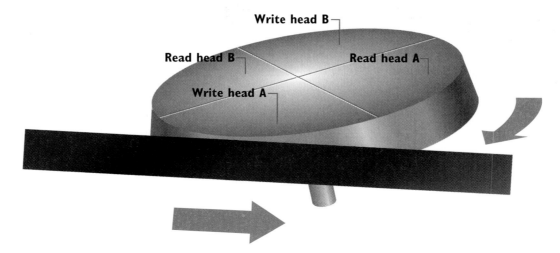

2 The distinctive design of the DAT drive's read/write head is what allows it to back up huge amounts of data onto a small tape cartridge about the size of a matchbox. The mechanism is a rotating cylinder with four heads 90 degrees apart. Two of these heads, write heads A and B, write backup data, and two corresponding read heads verify the data. The cylinder tilts slightly so it rotates at an angle to the tape. The cylinder spins 2,000 times a minute while the tape (at a rate of ½ inch a second) passes in front of the cylinder in the opposite direction of the cylinder's spin.

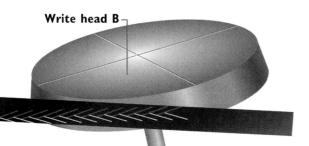

5 As write head B passes over the tape, it writes data in a track at a 40-degree angle to track A, making a crisscross pattern that overlaps track A. The overlapping data packs more information per inch of tape; it isn't misread later because the magnetic bits written by the two write heads have different polarities, and the different read heads read data only from properly aligned tracks.

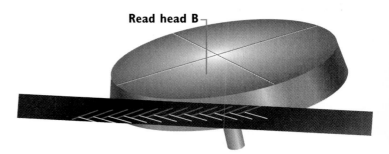

6 Read head B and write head B go through the same steps, alternating with the A heads until all the data is backed up. Then the drive rewinds the tape and writes a directory of stored files either in a special partition at the front of the tape or in a file on the hard disk.

NOTE When you restore files from the DAT drive, the software reads the directory, winds the tape to the spot where the requested files begin, and copies the files to the hard disk.

P A R T

INPUT/OUTPUT DEVICES

ALL the marvelous tasks that a personal computer is capable of doing would be meaningless without some way for the PC to communicate with the world outside of itself. The first personal computers, such as the Altair, used a method of communicating so primitive that it's a wonder computing pioneers had the imagination to conceive that these contraptions could be practical in the real world. Program instructions and data were fed into the computer by flipping electrical switches—not miniaturized switches in the form of transistors but ordinary thumb-sized switches. The results of a computation were presented in the form of a seemingly random pattern of tiny light bulbs lit on a panel.

Today, the ways in which we communicate with a PC encompass devices that even the more imaginative of personal computing pioneers didn't envision. Keyboards and cathode-ray tubes (CRTs) are so common that we can't imagine a PC without them. In addition, there are modems, scanners, mice, and digital cameras, which help us obtain information and instructions from the outside world. In addition to the common CRT, there are a wide variety of state-of-the-art displays, including SuperVGA and active matrix color, and printers capable of far more than tapping out crude letters. So, today, you have a personal computer that is part of the real world, something you treat more like a person—someone who listens and replies to you—than you'd treat any other collection of microchips and electronics.

Strictly speaking, most devices outside the microprocessor itself—the largest part of a PC, in other words—are input or output devices. Each act of reading or writing data on a disk drive or in memory uses the services of the computer's BIOS (Basic Input/Output System). Still, we tend to associate input and output only with the devices, such as keyboard, monitor, and mouse, that we can see and touch. Our myopic view of what makes up input and output devices is understandable, for without those devices, even the most powerful PC imaginable would be nothing more than an awkward tool for the dedicated and a curiosity for the rest of us.

CHAPTER

14

How a Bus Works

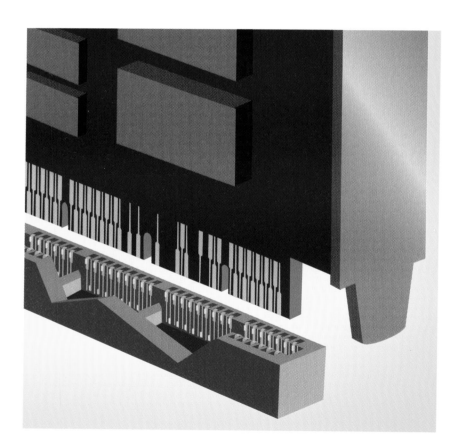

WE usually think of input and output (I/O) as ways for us to communicate with our computers. That may be true from our viewpoint, but as far as your PC is concerned, it's got a lot more I/O to worry about than just yours. Millions of bits of information are constantly flashing among the components of your PC even when it appears to be simply sitting there. Various traffic cops called input/output controllers work with the processor to make sure that all this data swapping doesn't cause a traffic jam, or worse still, a crash.

The *bus* is the highway system for this data. The bus transports data among the processor and other components. There is no single part of the PC's motherboard you can point to and say it's the bus. The bus is a complex conglomeration of electrical circuits called *traces*. Traces are printed on the top and bottom of the motherboard, which is the main circuit board in your PC. The bus also includes assorted microchips, and the slots into which we plug expansion circuit boards—often called *adapters* or *expansion cards*. Sometimes the bus is called the *expansion bus*, and the slots lined with dozens of metallic contacts are called *expansion* or *adapter slots*.

The idea of having slots into which you can plug other circuit boards that work with the main motherboard is one of the best features of personal computers. Without the slots, you'd be stuck with whatever video, disk controller, and other circuitry that were permanently wired into the motherboard. For example, expansion slots allow you to remove one card that controls the video display and replace it with a new video card that handles Windows graphics faster. You can even add circuit boards, such as sound cards, that weren't even imagined when your PC was built. Today there's a trend toward making some components, such as parallel ports, serial ports, and video controllers, part of the motherboard. But in the case of, for example, an integrated video controller, it can be disabled if you want to install an expansion card that handles video better.

The basic idea of the bus introduced on the IBM PC in 1981 was so good and so versatile that for years, there were few changes. But today there are a half dozen types of PC buses. All of them represent improvements in moving data still faster among components.

The first change in the original PC bus was to increase its ability to move only 8 bits of data at a time. When IBM introduced the IBM AT computer in 1984, the new system included expansion slots with more connectors to send 16 bits of data at a time—twice as much information as the original bus. This bus, called ISA, for Industry Standard Architecture, is the most common, still appearing in most new PCs today, although usually in combination with other types of expansion slots.

The ISA expansion slots have the advantage that you can still plug older 8-bit adapters into them. The older cards simply use fewer of the slots' connectors. But in 1987 IBM introduced the PS/2 computer, with a radically different type of bus, which IBM called the Microchannel Architecture, or MCA. It handles 32 bits of data at a time, and it has a primitive intelligence to allow it to adjust to the rest of your system automatically. This helps eliminate conflicts caused when two components want to use the same system resources, such as the location, or address, in memory.

MCA was a good idea. But it never really caught on for two reasons. First, it wouldn't accept the older 8-bit and 16-bit ISA expansion cards, and PC owners didn't like the idea of abandoning perfectly good adapters. Second, IBM originally didn't let other companies clone the bus as IBM had permitted with the earlier bus designs. Without other companies behind MCA, not only did the design languish, but it also inspired a countermove by seven IBM competitors. Led by Compaq, in 1988 the rivals introduced the EISA (Extended Industry Standard Architecture) bus. It provided the faster, 32-bit data flow and autoconfiguration of MCA, but a clever slot design lets it also use ISA cards. But EISA is complex and expensive, and it has never caught on except for use on high-end systems where every drop of speed counts.

In 1992 computer manufacturers came up with a new twist in bus design. Previously, they had concentrated on making buses push more bits of data at one time—from 8 to 16 to 32 bits. But even EISA and MCA buses were still operating, respectively, at 8.22 and 10 megahertz (MHz), despite the release of newer processors capable of churning out data at 33MHz or faster. To bring the bus up to speed, the local bus was created. "Local" refers to bus lines used by the processor. (If you think of the bus lines as being located in the *neighborhood* of the processor, then the term "local" makes a bit more sense.) Some of those local bus lines lead to expansion slots, giving the slot local, or direct, access to the processor. The advantage of the local bus is that it theoretically communicates with the processor at the processor's own speed. In reality, the speed for now is less, but still a terrific improvement over ISA. Typically, local bus expansion slots exist side by side with ISA slots, and the local bus slots are used for components, such as video and drive controller cards, that most affect the overall performance of the computer because they move enormous amounts of data.

There are two versions of the local bus. The Video Electronics Standards Association (VESA) is an alliance of PC vendors who developed the VESA local bus, or VL-Bus, to accelerate video displays with working speeds up to 50MHz. Intel Corporation and other big PC companies developed the PCI (Peripheral Component Interconnect) local bus. Although

PCI permits speeds up to only 33MHz, PCI local bus is a more comprehensive design that is the first to incorporate Plug and Play setup. Despite its slow bus speed, currently the PCI local bus is capable of moving a maximum of 132 megabytes a second, compared to the VESA transmission rate of 107MB/sec and to the ISA transmission rate of 8MB a second. Both VESA and PCI are being revamped, but PCI is more likely to become the de facto local bus standard.

Differences in Expansion Cards

8–bit Expansion Card Data is transmitted among expansion slots and other components on the bus only along 8 parallel data lines. The data lines use only a fraction of the 31 pairs of connectors that fit into the expansion slot. As remains the same with newer boards, the other connectors supply the board with power, instructions, and addresses for data locations either on the expansion boards or in memory.

16–bit or ISA Card With 18 more pairs of connectors, the ISA (Industry Standard Architecture) card transmits data over 16 data lines, doubling the amount of data it moves compared to an 8-bit card. This is the most prevalent type of expansion card, and even PCs with faster and newer local bus slots still have ISA expansion slots. A 16-bit card is powerful enough for components, such as keyboards, serial and parallel ports, and internal modems that don't handle the extreme amounts of data transmitted by video, network, and disk controller cards.

32-bit MCA Card The IBM Microchannel (MCA) card uses 32 of its 93 lines to send and receive data. It also includes special circuitry that, like Plug and Play technology (see Chapter 3), makes the card easier to install. The MCA expansion slot, which IBM refused to let others clone for a long time, will not accept 8-bit or ISA adapter cards.

32-bit EISA Card The design of Extended Industry Standard Architecture (EISA) can use expansions cards designed specifically to work with the slot's 97 connectors that are divided between two levels. These EISA-specific cards transmit 32 bits of data at a time and, like MCA and Plug and Play, are easier to set up. But EISA slots also accept 8-bit and 16-bit cards. Plastic tabs allow the older cards to fit only far enough into the slots to make contact with the first level of connectors, which work the same as ISA connections. But boards designed specifically for the EISA slot can enter farther and align their connectors with the lower row of connectors that handle signals based on EISA specifications.

32-bit VESA Local-bus (VL-Bus) Card Cards designed for the Video Electronics Standards Association (VESA) local-bus slots are divided into a set of connectors based on the ISA slot and a separate set of 36 more pairs of smaller connectors that carry the local bus information. The VL-Bus cards work with 32-bit data.

32-bit PCI Local-bus Card The PCI (Peripheral Component Interconnect) local bus adapters have connectors similar to those on MCA and EISA cards. All handle 32 bits of data at a time, and are smaller and more tightly packed than ISA connections. But PCI slots won't accept ISA or 8-bit cards.

Local Bus

VESA Local Bus

1 Signals from the microprocessor are first sent to an I/O (Input/Output) controller that handles VL-bus operations. The signals include some code that supplies an address that is the intended destination for the rest of the signals.

2 The controller decodes the address signals from the processor to determine if the signals are intended for any of the local-bus adapters.

3 Signals going to nonlocal bus adapters are passed on to the ISA I/O controller, which normally handles nonlocal bus operations, 16 bits at a time at a speed of about 8MHz.

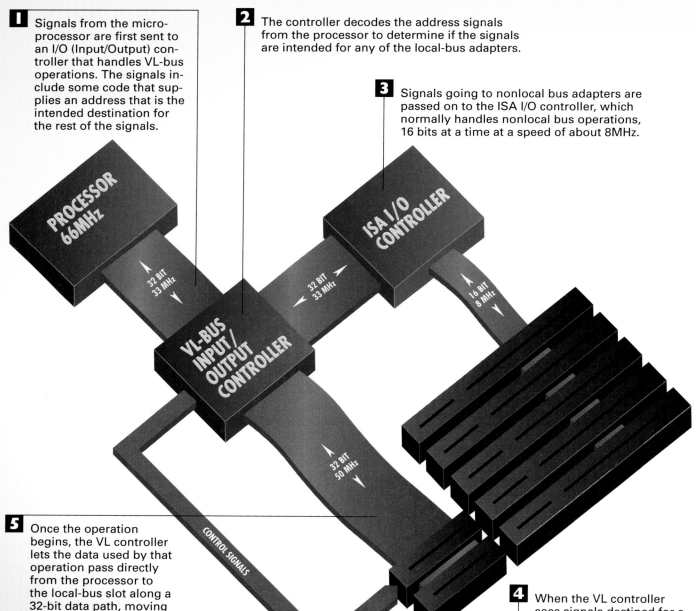

5 Once the operation begins, the VL controller lets the data used by that operation pass directly from the processor to the local-bus slot along a 32-bit data path, moving at speeds up to 50MHz.

4 When the VL controller sees signals destined for a local-bus slot, it sends a control signal to the adapter in that slot, telling it to execute the operation requested by the signals.

PCI Local Bus

2 The PCI controller examines all signals from the microprocessor to determine if the intended address for the signals is a local-bus adapter or a nonlocal bus adapter.

3 The PCI controller routes all signals meant for a nonlocal bus adapter to a second controller, usually an ISA controller, although it could be a controller for an MCA or EISA bus. This part of the bus moves data 16 bits at a time for ISA circuits, and 32 bits at a time for EISA or MCA circuits. The speed of these signals is limited to about 8–10MHz.

1 Signals from the processor go to an I/O controller for PCI local bus operations. The controller sits between the processor and the normal ISA controller.

PROCESSOR 66mHz

32 BIT 33 MHz

32 BIT 33 MHz

ISA I/O CONTROLLER

16 BIT 8 MHz

PCI-BUS I/O CONTROLLER

32 BIT 33 MHz

4 The controller routes all signals being sent to local bus components along one path leading to the local bus adapter slots. Data on this path travels 32 bits at a time at speeds up to 33MHz.

CHAPTER

15

How a Keyboard Works

YOU come into direct contact with your PC's keyboard more than you do with any other component. You may go for years without ever seeing—much less touching—your PC's processor or hard drive, but most people pay much more attention to those components than they do to the one part of the computer that determines not how well the computer works but how well they work.

A poorly designed keyboard acts as a constant stumbling block to productivity and can even cause health problems. A well-designed keyboard is one that you never think about; your thoughts seem to flow directly from your mind to the computer's screen without you being aware of what your fingers are doing.

Despite the importance of the keyboard, most manufacturers—and too many users—pay little attention to it. Some keyboards these days are equipped with built-in trackballs or some other sort of pointing device, and some keyboards offer different slopes, which designers hope will help avoid repetitive-motion syndrome. The few radical changes that have appeared—concave keyboards with their keys equidistant from the fingers or keyboards that can be operated with one hand—have not caught on.

Regardless of whether it's because manufacturers are unimaginative or that computer users just don't care, the basic way a keyboard works has not changed significantly since the first IBM PC was introduced in the early 1980s. Although the layout of all keys except the alphanumeric ones is up for grabs—particularly on notebook keyboards—the only practical difference in how keyboards work is the mechanism that converts a key cap's movement into a signal sent to the computer. Except for this difference, the movement of the signal through the rest of the keyboard and your PC is a time-tested technology.

The Keyboard and Scan Codes

3 Depending on which key's circuit carries a signal to the microprocessor, the processor generates a number, called a *scan code*. There are two scan codes for each key, one for when the key is depressed and the other for when it's released. The processor stores the number in the keyboard's own memory buffer, and it loads the number in a port connection where it can be read by the computer's BIOS. Then the processor sends an interrupt signal over the keyboard cable to tell the processor that a scan code is waiting for it. An interrupt tells the processor to drop whatever else it is doing and to divert its attention to the service requested by the interrupt.

2 A microprocessor, such as the Intel 8048, built into the keyboard constantly scans circuits leading to the key caps. It detects the increase or decrease in current from the key that has been pressed. By detecting either an increase or a decrease in current, the processor can tell both when a key has been pressed and when it's been released. Each key has a unique set of codes, even if to the users, the keys seem identical. The processor can, for example, distinguish between the left and right shift keys. To distinguish between a real signal and an aberrant current fluctuation, the scan is repeated hundreds of times each second. Only signals detected for two or more scans are acted upon by the processor.

1 Regardless of which type of key cap is used, pressing it causes a change in the current flowing though the circuits associated with that key cap.

INTEL 8048

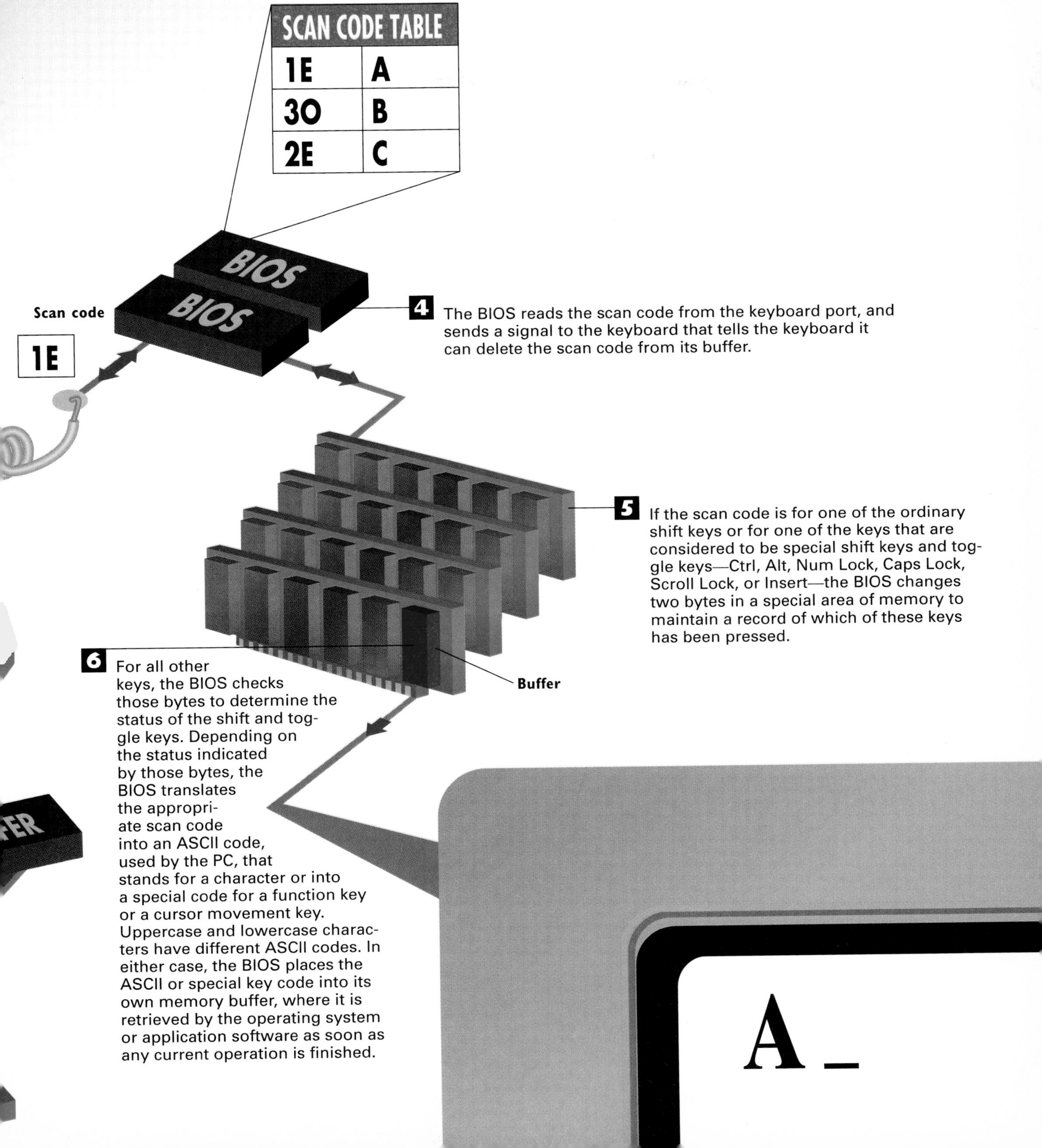

SCAN CODE TABLE

1E	A
30	B
2E	C

Scan code

1E

BIOS

BIOS

4 The BIOS reads the scan code from the keyboard port, and sends a signal to the keyboard that tells the keyboard it can delete the scan code from its buffer.

5 If the scan code is for one of the ordinary shift keys or for one of the keys that are considered to be special shift keys and toggle keys—Ctrl, Alt, Num Lock, Caps Lock, Scroll Lock, or Insert—the BIOS changes two bytes in a special area of memory to maintain a record of which of these keys has been pressed.

Buffer

6 For all other keys, the BIOS checks those bytes to determine the status of the shift and toggle keys. Depending on the status indicated by those bytes, the BIOS translates the appropriate scan code into an ASCII code, used by the PC, that stands for a character or into a special code for a function key or a cursor movement key. Uppercase and lowercase characters have different ASCII codes. In either case, the BIOS places the ASCII or special key code into its own memory buffer, where it is retrieved by the operating system or application software as soon as any current operation is finished.

A _

CHAPTER

16

How a Computer Display Works

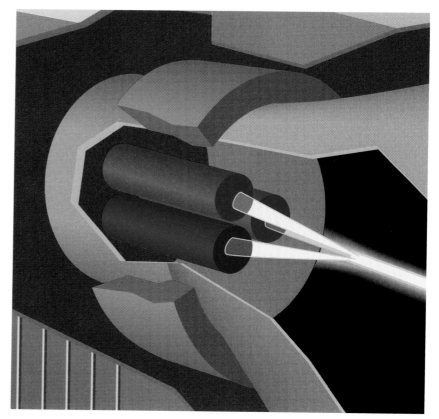

A few years ago, color monitors for personal computers were considered frivolous—more suited for playing games than doing real work. Most software was text based, and text produced by color displays was crude and difficult to read. Even for graphics applications, the color graphics adapter (CGA) monitors, which were the first color displays to appear for DOS-based computers, were seriously hindered by their inability to display more than 4 colors from a possible 16 in the monitor's highest resolution—a resolution filled with zigzags instead of smooth curves and straight lines.

Today, all that's changed. Not only is color considered acceptable for serious computing, but it's preferable in a computing arena that, with environments such as Windows and OS/2, is increasingly graphic. Software today uses color not simply to make itself prettier, but to convey more information.

Today's color displays are a far cry from the limited, crude color and graphics of only a decade ago. Instead of 4 colors, a palette of at least 256 colors is commonplace, and some displays provide thousands of colors. Instead of the CGA's Etch-a-Sketch–type resolution of 200 lines high by 640 pixels wide, modern displays provide resolutions of 768 lines high by 1,024 pixels wide without breaking a sweat. (A *pixel*, short for *picture element*, is the smallest logical unit that can be used to build an image on the screen. A single pixel is usually created by several adjoining points of light. The fewer the dots of light used to create a pixel, the higher a monitor's resolution.)

The secret of today's better displays is a combination of the variable-graphics-array (VGA) display adapter and versatile monitors that can work with a variety of signals from the display adapter. Older display adapters used digital information exclusively, which meant that a display's pixel was either on or off, making it difficult to achieve subtle distinctions in colors. VGA uses an analog signal that converts digital information into different voltage levels that vary the brightness of a pixel. The process requires less memory and is more versatile. Super VGA displays use special chip sets and bigger memory to increase the number of colors and resolution even more.

Some form of VGA will be the standard for years to come. Here, we'll look at two types of VGA color displays—a desktop monitor and an LCD screen on a portable PC.

VGA Desktop Monitor

2 The DAC compares the digital values sent by the PC to a look-up table that contains the matching voltage levels for the three primary colors needed to create the color of a single pixel. The table contains values for 262,144 possible colors, of which 256 values can be stored in the VGA adapter's memory at one time. (Super VGA displays, which have more memory, can handle more colors and, for higher resolution, more pixels.)

VOLTAGES			
RED	GREEN	BLUE	
5	2.5	1	
5	2.5	2	
5	2.5	3	
5	2.5	4	
5	2.5	5	

3 The adapter sends signals to three electron guns located at the back of the monitor's cathode-ray tube (CRT). Through the vacuum inside the CRT, each electron gun shoots out a stream of electrons, one stream for each of the three primary colors. The intensity of each stream is controlled by the signals from the adapter.

4 The adapter also sends signals to a mechanism in the neck of the CRT that focuses and aims the electron beams. The mechanism, a *magnetic deflection yoke*, uses electromagnetic fields to bend the path of the electron streams. The signals sent to the yoke help determine the monitor's resolution—the number of pixels horizontally and vertically—and the monitor's *refresh rate*, which is how frequently the screen's image is redrawn.

DAC

1 Digital signals from the operating environment or application software are received by the VGA adapter (sometimes built into the PC's motherboard). The adapter runs the signals through a circuit called a *digital-to-analog converter* (DAC). Usually the DAC circuit is contained within one specialized chip, which actually contains three DACs—one for each of the primary colors used in a display: red, blue, and green.

5 The beams pass through holes in a metal plate called a *shadow mask*. The purpose of the mask is to keep the electron beams precisely aligned with their targets on the inside of the CRT's screen. The CRT's *dot pitch* is the measurement of how close the holes are to each other; the closer the holes, the smaller the dot pitch. This, in turn, creates a sharper image. The holes in most shadow masks are arranged in triangles, with the important exception of those of the Sony Trinitron CRT used by many monitor manufacturers. The Trinitron's holes are arranged as parallel slots.

6 The electrons strike the phosphors coating the inside of the screen. *Phosphors* are materials that glow when they are struck by electrons. Three different phosphor materials are used—one each for red, blue, and green. The stronger the electron beam that hits a phosphor, the more light the phosphor emits. If each red, green, and blue dot in an arrangement is struck by equally intense electron beams, the result is a dot of white light. To create different colors, the intensity of each of the three beams is varied. After a beam leaves a phosphor dot, the phosphor continues to glow briefly, a condition called *persistence*. For an image to remain stable, the phosphors must be reactivated by repeated scans of the electron beams.

7 After the beams make one horizontal sweep across the screen, the electron streams are turned off as the electron guns refocus the path of the beams back to the left edge of the screen at a point just below the previous scan line. The process is called *raster scanning*.

8 The *magnetic deflection yoke* continually changes the angles at which the electron beams are bent so that they sweep across the entire screen surface from the upper-left corner of the screen to the lower-right corner. A complete sweep of the screen is called a *field*. Upon completing a field, the beams return to the upper-left corner to begin a new field. The screen is normally redrawn, or refreshed, about 60 times a second.

9 Some display adapters scan only every other line with each field, a process called *interlacing*. Interlacing allows the adapter to create higher resolutions—that is, to scan more lines—with less expensive components. But the fading of the phosphors between each pass can be noticeable, causing the screen to flicker.

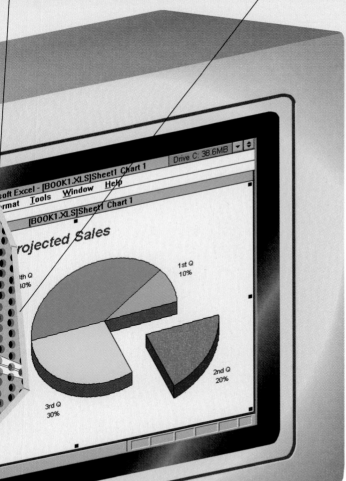

Color Liquid Crystal Display

3 In a layer of liquid-crystal cells, the built-in graphics adapter of the portable PC applies a varying electrical charge to some of the cells and no charge at all to other cells. In cells to which current is applied, the long, rod-shaped molecules that make up the liquid-crystal material react to the charge by forming a spiral. The greater the charge, the more that the molecules spiral. With the strongest charge, the molecules at one end of the cell wind up at an angle 90 degrees from the orientation of the molecules at the other end of the cell.

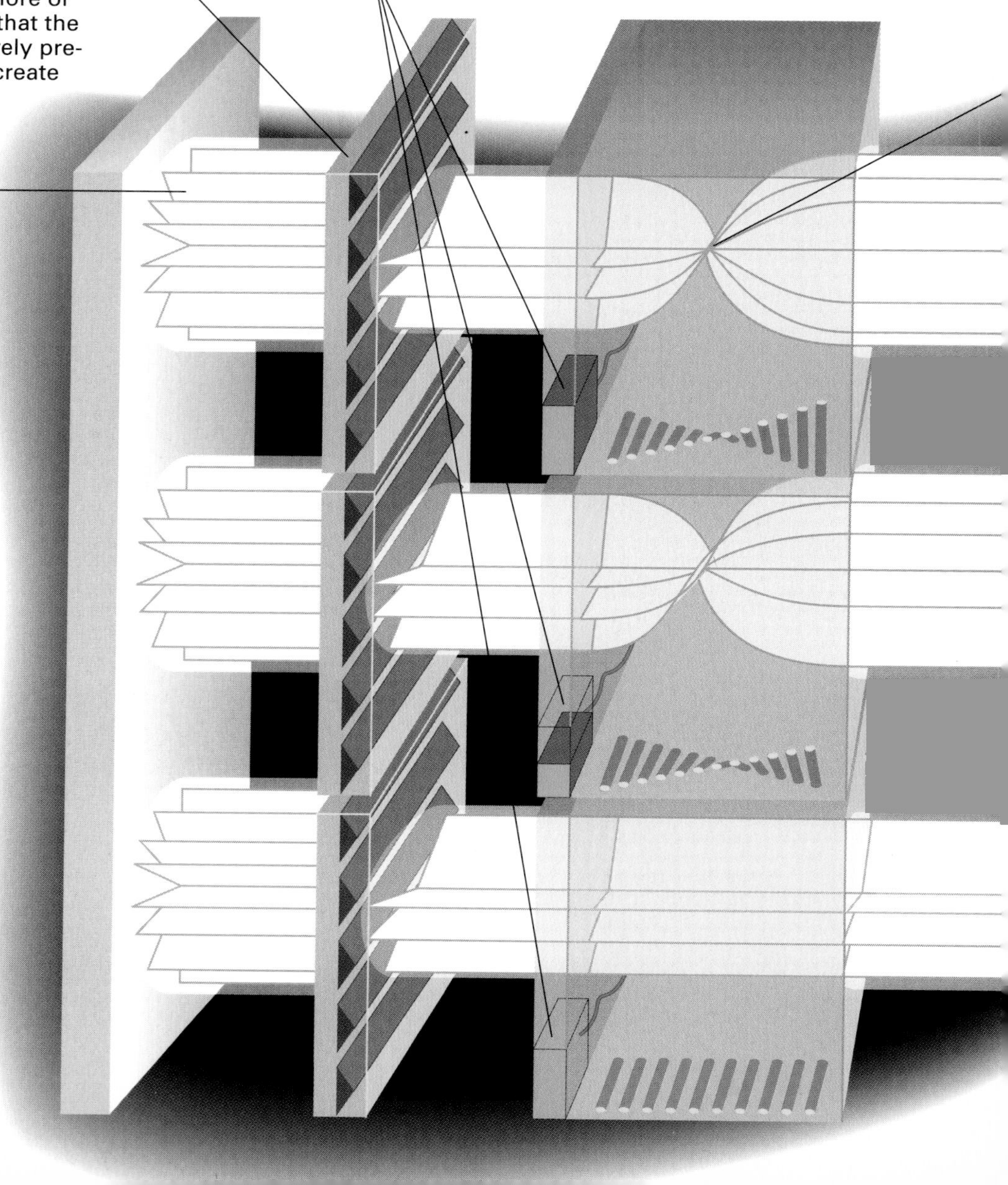

2 A polarizing filter in front of the light panel lets through only the light waves that are vibrating more or less horizontally. The fact that the polarizing filter is not entirely precise allows the display to create different hues.

1 Light—emanating from a fluorescent panel behind a portable computer's display panel—spreads out in waves that vibrate in all directions.

NOTE The model shown here is only one way in which liquid crystals and polarizers can manipulate light. Some LCD panels use two polarizers with the same alignment so that a charge applied to a liquid crystal cell results in light that's blocked because it's twisted. Also, two methods are used to apply charges to liquid crystal cells. Passive matrix displays use only a relatively few electrodes arranged as strips along the liquid crystal layer and rely on timing to make sure the correct cells are charged. The charges in passive matrix cells fade quickly, causing the colors to look faded. Active matrix displays, such as the one shown here, have individual transistors for each of the cells. The individual transistors provide a more precise and stronger charge, creating colors that are more vivid.

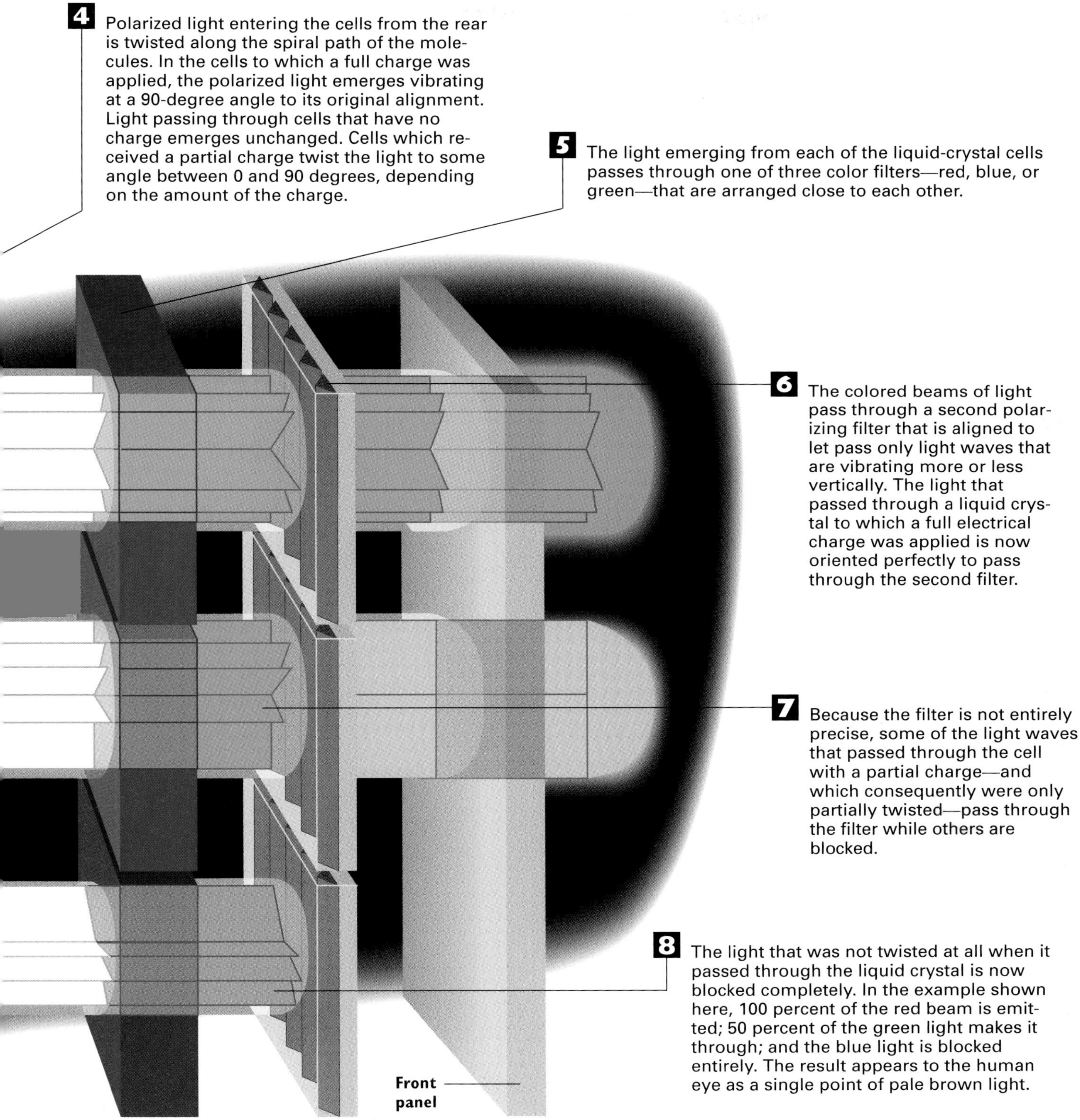

4 Polarized light entering the cells from the rear is twisted along the spiral path of the molecules. In the cells to which a full charge was applied, the polarized light emerges vibrating at a 90-degree angle to its original alignment. Light passing through cells that have no charge emerges unchanged. Cells which received a partial charge twist the light to some angle between 0 and 90 degrees, depending on the amount of the charge.

5 The light emerging from each of the liquid-crystal cells passes through one of three color filters—red, blue, or green—that are arranged close to each other.

6 The colored beams of light pass through a second polarizing filter that is aligned to let pass only light waves that are vibrating more or less vertically. The light that passed through a liquid crystal to which a full electrical charge was applied is now oriented perfectly to pass through the second filter.

7 Because the filter is not entirely precise, some of the light waves that passed through the cell with a partial charge—and which consequently were only partially twisted—pass through the filter while others are blocked.

8 The light that was not twisted at all when it passed through the liquid crystal is now blocked completely. In the example shown here, 100 percent of the red beam is emitted; 50 percent of the green light makes it through; and the blue light is blocked entirely. The result appears to the human eye as a single point of pale brown light.

Front panel

CHAPTER 17

How a Serial Port Works

WITHOUT

a computer's serial and parallel ports, much of the work that a PC accomplishes would never reach anyone other than the person sitting in front of the monitor. The serial port is the jack-of-all-trades among computer components. It is simple in concept: one line to send data, another line to receive data, and a few other lines to regulate how data is sent over the other two lines. Because of its simplicity, the serial port has been used at one time or another to make a PC communicate with just about any device imaginable—from commonplace modems and printers to plotters and burglar alarms.

The most common uses for a serial port are with a mouse or modem. The reason for this is that a serial port is not a very efficient way to transfer data. It can only send data in series—one bit of data at a time, rather like soldiers marching single file. This inefficient data transfer, however, is acceptable for mice, which transmit so little data that speed is not crucial, and perfect for modems because the most common phone lines cannot transport more than one signal at a time anyway.

The serial port is often referred to as an RS-232 port. RS-232 is the Electronics Industries Association's designation for a standard for how the various connectors in a serial port are to be used. The trouble is that the standard is sometimes ignored by manufacturers of peripherals and even computer makers. The fact that both 9-pin and 25-pin connectors are used as serial ports shows we still have a long way to go before settling on exactly what constitutes an RS-232 port. The example shown here, which uses both types of connectors, depicts a serial port—connected to a modem—that conforms to the RS-232 standard.

Serial Port

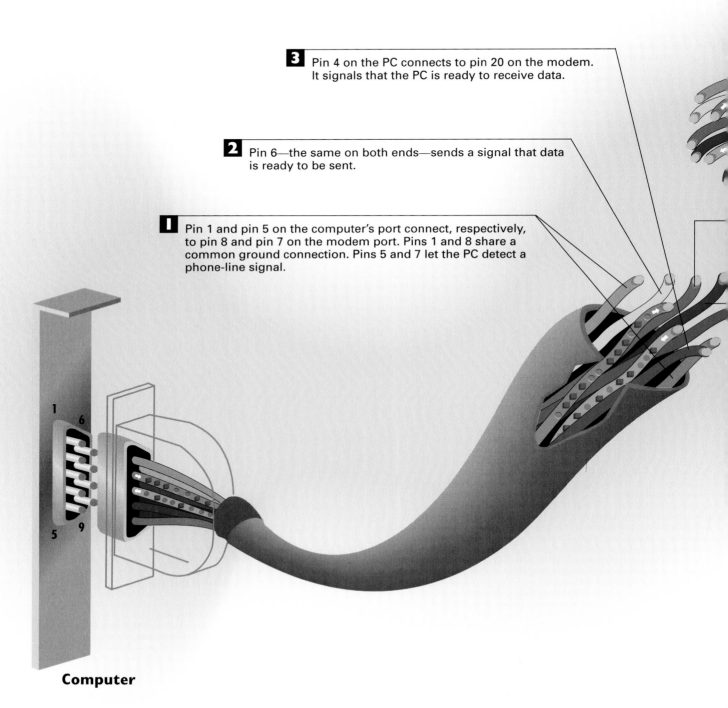

3 Pin 4 on the PC connects to pin 20 on the modem. It signals that the PC is ready to receive data.

2 Pin 6—the same on both ends—sends a signal that data is ready to be sent.

1 Pin 1 and pin 5 on the computer's port connect, respectively, to pin 8 and pin 7 on the modem port. Pins 1 and 8 share a common ground connection. Pins 5 and 7 let the PC detect a phone-line signal.

Computer

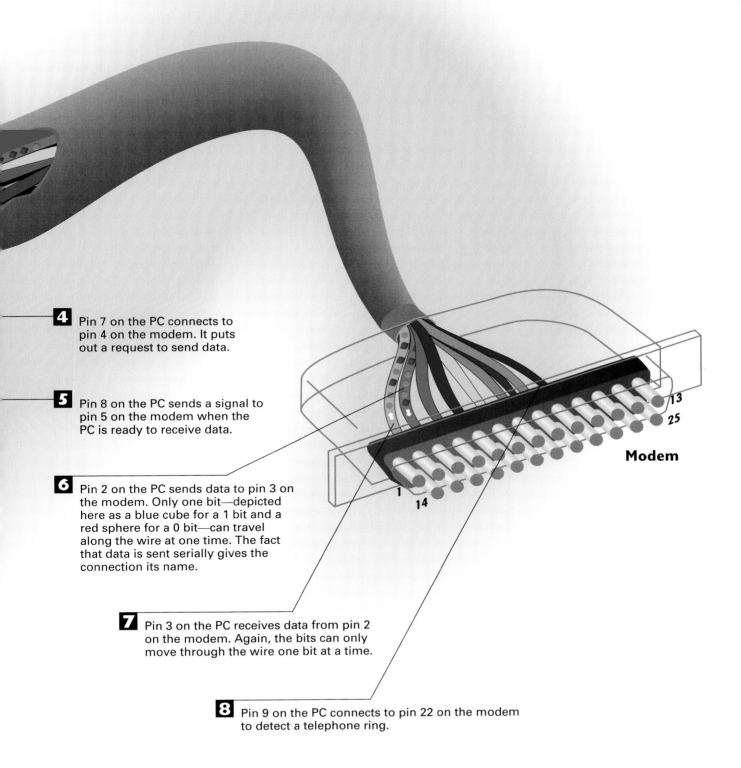

4 Pin 7 on the PC connects to pin 4 on the modem. It puts out a request to send data.

5 Pin 8 on the PC sends a signal to pin 5 on the modem when the PC is ready to receive data.

6 Pin 2 on the PC sends data to pin 3 on the modem. Only one bit—depicted here as a blue cube for a 1 bit and a red sphere for a 0 bit—can travel along the wire at one time. The fact that data is sent serially gives the connection its name.

7 Pin 3 on the PC receives data from pin 2 on the modem. Again, the bits can only move through the wire one bit at a time.

8 Pin 9 on the PC connects to pin 22 on the modem to detect a telephone ring.

Modem

13
25
1
14

CHAPTER

18

How a Parallel Port Works

SINCE its introduction, the *parallel port*—also called a Centronics port—has been almost synonymous with *printer port*. Although a serial port can also be used to send data from a PC to some models of printers, the parallel port is faster. A serial port sends data one bit at a time over a single one-way wire; a parallel port can send several bits of data across eight parallel wires simultaneously, like soldiers marching several abreast. In the same time that a serial connection sends a single bit, a parallel port can send an entire byte. Or another way to look at it: In the time a serial connection can send the letter A, a parallel port can send the word *aardvark*.

A parallel connection has one drawback. The voltages in all its lines create *cross talk*, a condition in which the voltages leak from one line to another, just as you can sometimes hear someone else's phone conversation that has leaked into your own phone connection. Cross talk becomes worse the longer a parallel cable is; this limits most parallel connections to 10 feet.

Some early printers and plotters used serial ports to communicate with a printer. But today, graphics and scalable fonts are common in printed documents and they require that vast amounts of data be sent to the printer, making a parallel port the only practical choice. In addition, parallel ports are used for transporting files between two PCs, and the popularity of portable computers—which often lack any expansion slots—has created a market for peripherals such as drives and sound generators that can work off parallel ports. Built-in circuitry and PC Cards, however, are quickly taking over many of the tasks parallel ports have been used for in laptops.

Parallel Port

1 A signal to the PC on line 13—called the *select line*—from the peripheral, usually a printer, tells the computer that the printer is on line and ready to receive data.

2 Data is loaded on lines 2 through 9 in the form of a high voltage—actually about five volts—to signify a 1, shown here as a blue cube, and a zero or a low nearly zero voltage to signify a 0, shown as a red sphere.

3 After the voltages have been set on all the data lines, line 1 sends a strobe signal to the printer for one microsecond to let the printer know that it should read the voltages on the data lines.

Computer

10 A signal from the PC on line 17 tells the printer not to accept data. This line is used only with some printers, which are designed to be switched on and off by the PC.

9 A low-voltage or zero-voltage signal from the PC on line 14 tells the printer to advance the paper one line when it receives a carriage return code. A high-voltage signal tells the printer to advance the paper one line only when it receives a line-advance code from the printer.

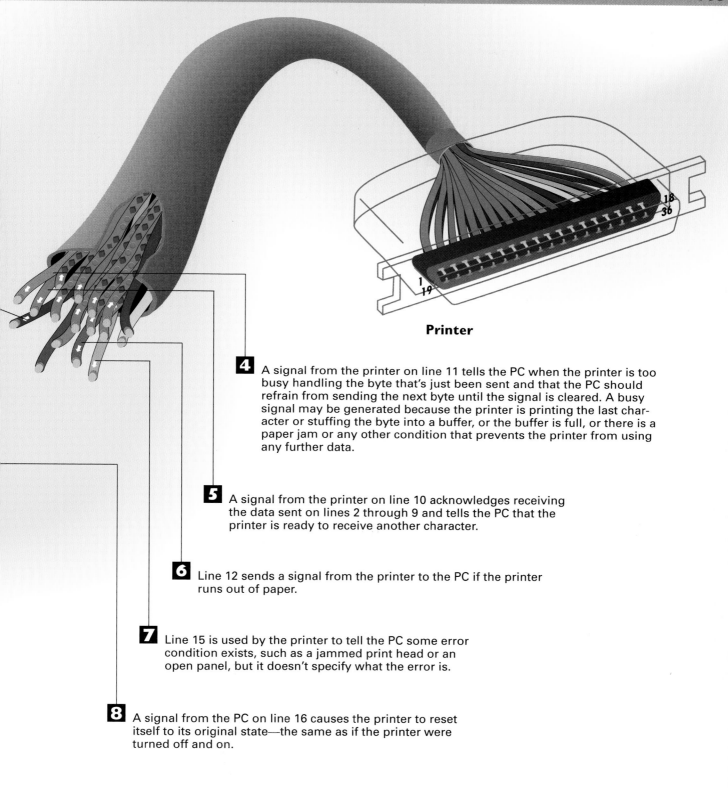

Printer

4 A signal from the printer on line 11 tells the PC when the printer is too busy handling the byte that's just been sent and that the PC should refrain from sending the next byte until the signal is cleared. A busy signal may be generated because the printer is printing the last character or stuffing the byte into a buffer, or the buffer is full, or there is a paper jam or any other condition that prevents the printer from using any further data.

5 A signal from the printer on line 10 acknowledges receiving the data sent on lines 2 through 9 and tells the PC that the printer is ready to receive another character.

6 Line 12 sends a signal from the printer to the PC if the printer runs out of paper.

7 Line 15 is used by the printer to tell the PC some error condition exists, such as a jammed print head or an open panel, but it doesn't specify what the error is.

8 A signal from the PC on line 16 causes the printer to reset itself to its original state—the same as if the printer were turned off and on.

NOTE Lines 18 through 25 are simply ground lines.

CHAPTER

19

How a Mouse Works

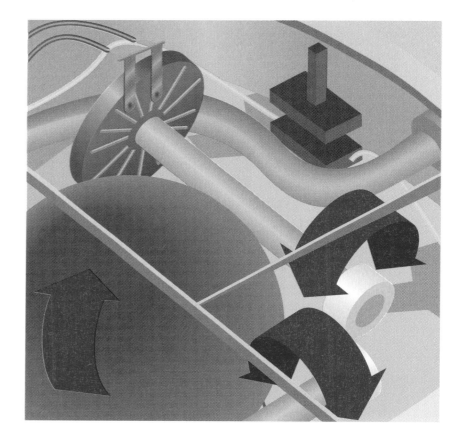

THERE is nothing natural or intuitive about a keyboard. No child is born knowing how to type, and even when the skill is learned, there's little sense to it—no one can give a sensible explanation of why the alphanumeric keys are arranged the way they are.

For many, the keyboard is a barrier to learning how to use a computer. Even for the experienced typist, there's nothing intuitive in typing /FS to save a file in Lotus 1-2-3 for DOS. Engineers—not one of them touch typists, we'll bet—at Xerox Corporation's Palo Alto Research Center (PARC) developed a concept first explored by Douglas C. Engelbert of the Stanford Research Center. The concept was a *pointing device*, something a computer user could move with his or her hand, causing a corresponding move on screen. Because of its size and taillike cable, the device was named for the mouse. Apple Computer made the mouse a standard feature of its Macintosh computers, and with the popularity of Windows, a mouse has become standard equipment on all PCs, as well.

The mouse is not the only pointing device that's been invented. The joy stick used with games essentially accomplishes the same task, but doesn't feel quite right in all situations. Digitizing tablets are popular with architects and engineers who must translate precise movements of a pen into lines on the screen. Touch screens, on which you press either your finger or a special light pen to control the software, are too tiring to use for any length of time.

The mouse and its cousin, the trackball, have survived those other, more awkward methods of navigating with the keyboard. Mice can never replace the keyboard, but they can supplement the keyboard by doing tasks such as moving and pointing to on-screen objects, tasks for which the cursor keys are ill-suited. Until we reach the point where we simply talk to our PCs, mice will be an integral part of our systems.

The mechanical mouse has become the most popular pointing device for the newest breed of operating environments—graphic interfaces represented by Windows, the Macintosh, and OS/2. With the mouse, you control your PC by pointing to images instead of typing in commands. Here's how the mouse translates the movements of your hand into the actions on screen.

Mechanical Mouse

4 On the rims of each encoder are tiny metal contact points. Two pairs of contact bars extend from the housing of the mouse and touch the contact points on each of the encoders as they pass by. Each time a contact bar touches a point, an electrical signal results. The number of signals indicates how many points the contact bars have touched—the more signals, the farther you have moved the mouse. The direction in which the rollers are turning, combined with the ratio between the number of signals from the vertical and horizontal rollers, indicate the direction that the mouse is moving.

3 Each roller is attached to a wheel, known as an *encoder*, much like a car's drivetrain is attached by its axles to the wheels. As the rollers turn, they rotate the encoders.

2 As the ball rotates, it touches and turns two rollers mounted at a 90-degree angle to each other. One roller responds to back-and-forth movements of the mouse, which correspond to vertical movements on screen. The other roller senses sideways movements, which correspond to side-to-side movements on screen.

1 As you move a mechanical mouse by dragging it across a flat surface, a ball—made of rubber or rubber over steel—protruding from the underside of the mouse turns in the direction of the movement.

5 Signals are sent to the PC over the mouse's tail-like cable to the software, which converts the number, combination, and frequency of signals from the two encoders into the distance, direction, and speed necessary to move the on-screen cursor.

6 Tapping either of the buttons atop the mouse also sends a signal to the PC, which passes the signal to the software. Based on how many times you click and the position of the cursor at the time of the click, the software performs the task you want to accomplish.

NOTE Want to know how a trackball works? Turn these pages upside-down and you'll get some idea. A trackball is simply a mouse mounted so that the ball is rotated with your fingers instead of on the surface of your desk.

CHAPTER 20

How a Modem Works

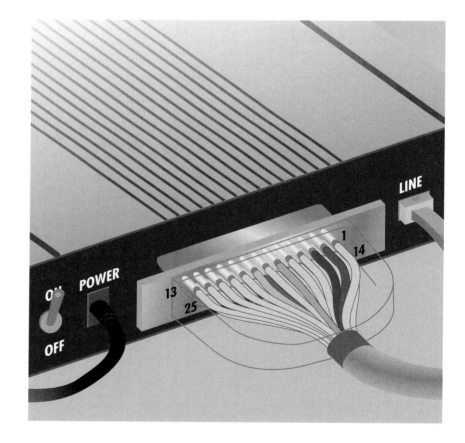

YOUR PC is a digital device. It accomplishes most of its tasks by turning on or off a series of electronic switches. A binary 0—shown here as a sphere—represents a switch that is turned off; a binary 1—a cube here—indicates that the switch is on. There is no in-between designation. A graph of digital code would look like this:

The telephone system is an analog device, designed—at a time when digital electronics was unknown—to transmit the diverse sounds and tones of the human voice. Those sounds are conveyed electronically in an analog signal as a continuous electronic current that smoothly varies its frequency and strength. It can be depicted on an oscilloscope as a wavy line, such as this:

A *modem* is the bridge between digital and analog signals. It converts on and off digital data into an analog signal by varying, or modulating, the frequency of an electronic wave, a process similar to that used by FM radio stations. On the receiving end of a phone connection, a modem does just the opposite: It demodulates the analog signals back into digital code. The two terms *MOdulate* and *DEModulate* give the modem its name.

Modem communications involve three of the least standardized elements of personal computing—serial ports, modem commands, and communications software (see Chapter 17, "How a Serial Port Works"). The inconsistencies make it impossible to describe one universal way in which all modems work, but the operations discussed here accurately describe most software that uses a Hayes command-set modem with a 25-pin serial port.

Modem

1 Your communications software sends a voltage along pin 20 of the serial port to which the modem is connected. The voltage is called a *Data Terminal Ready* signal, or simply, a DTR signal. It tells the modem that the PC is turned on and ready to transmit data. At the same time, the PC detects a voltage from the modem on pin 6—*Data Set Ready*, or DSR signal—that lets the PC know the modem is ready to receive data or instructions. Both signals must be present before anything else can happen.

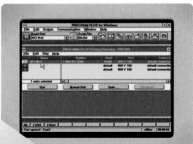

2 Using a standard command language named after the Hayes modems on which it was first popularized, the communications software sends a command to the modem via line 2, the Transmit Data line. The command tells your modem to go *off hook*—to open a connection with the phone line. The software follows with another Hayes command that tells the modem to issue the tones or pulses needed to dial a specific phone number. The modem acknowledges the command by replying to the PC on line 3, the Receive Data line.

4 When communications are established, your modem sends your PC a *Carrier Detect* (CD) signal on line 8. The signal tells the communications software that the modem is receiving a *carrier signal*, which is a steady tone of a certain frequency and which later will be modulated to transmit data.

3 When the modem on the other end of the phone connection—the remote modem—answers the call, your local modem sends out a hailing tone to let the remote modem know that it's being called by another modem. The remote modem responds with a higher-pitched tone. (You can ordinarily hear the two tones if your modem is equipped with a speaker.)

5 The two modems exchange information about how they'll send data to each other, a process called a *handshake*. The two modems must agree on the transfer speed, the number of bits that make up a *data packet*—for example, a single character—how many bits will signal the beginning and end of a packet, whether the modems will use a parity bit for error checking, and whether they will operate at *half-duplex* or *full duplex*. If the local and remote systems do not use the same settings, either they'll wind up sending characters that make no sense or they'll refuse to communicate at all.

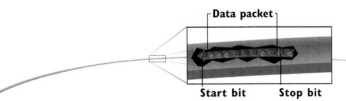

Frequency 1   Frequency 2   Frequency 3   Frequency 2

Transmission Speed Although transmission speeds are often expressed in *baud*—the number of frequency changes occurring during one second—that term is outdated and *bits per second* is more accurate today. The transmission rate on early modems of 300 bits per second was achieved by sending one frequency to indicate a 0 bit and a different frequency to indicate a 1 bit. The analog signal of a phone line, however, can't change frequencies more than 600 times a second. This is a serious limitation that affects the transmission rate. It has necessitated different schemes to increase the rate at which data is sent.

  Group coding permits different frequencies to stand for more than one bit at a time. For 1,200 bit-per-second transmissions, for example, signals are actually sent at 600 baud, but four different frequencies are used to represent the four different possible pairs of binary bits: 0 and 0, 0 and 1, 1 and 0, and 1 and 1. A similar scheme matches more frequencies with more binary combinations to achieve 2,400 bits per second. For still faster transmission rates, the two modems must both use the same method of compressing data by recognizing frequently repeated patterns of 0s and 1s and using shorter codes to stand for those patterns.

┌Data packet┐

Start bit   Stop bit

Start/Stop Bits Each data packet uses a single bit to signal the start of a character and either one bit or two bits to signal the end of a character. The example here uses one stop bit.

Parity Bit As a form of error correction, the two systems may agree to use even parity, odd parity, or no parity at all. If they agree on even or odd parity, both systems add up the bits contained in the character and then add another bit called the parity bit. It may be either a 0 bit or a 1 bit, whichever is needed, to make the total either an even number or an odd number, depending on the parity that the systems agree on. The parity bits are used for error checking.

Data Bits Communications systems may use either seven bits or eight bits to represent a data packet. In this example, eight data bits are used.

Half-/Full Duplex The two systems must agree which is responsible for displaying text on the local computer. One system must be set for full duplex and the other set for half-duplex. The system using full duplex is responsible for display text on both systems and echoes any text sent to it by the half-duplex system. If the two systems don't use complementary duplex settings, either no text will appear on the local system or each character will appear twice.

Modem

6 When the communications software wants to send data, it first sends voltage to line 4 on the serial port. This Request to Send (RTS) signal, in effect, asks if the modem is free to receive data from your PC. If the modem is receiving remote data it wants to pass on to your PC while your PC is busy doing something else, such as saving earlier data to disk, the PC will suspend the RTS signal to tell the modem to stop sending it data until the PC finishes its other work and reasserts the RTS signal

7 Unless your modem is too busy handling other data to receive new data from your system, it returns a Clear to Send (CTS) signal to your PC on serial port line 5, and your PC responds by sending the data to be transmitted on line 2. The modem sends data it received from the remote system to your PC via line 3. If the modem cannot transmit the data as fast as your PC sends data to it, the modem will drop the CTS signal to tell your PC to hold off on any further data until the modem catches up and renews the signal.

9 When you tell your communications software to end a communications session, the software sends another Hayes command to the modem that causes it to break the phone connection. If the connection is broken by the remote system, your modem will drop the Carrier Detect signal to your PC to tell the software that communications are broken.

8 At the other end of the phone line, the remote modem hears incoming data as a series of tones with different frequencies. It demodulates these tones back into digital signals and sends them to the receiving computer. Actually, both computers can send signals back and forth at the same time because the use of a standard system of tones allows modems on either end to distinguish between incoming and outgoing signals.

Reading Your Modem Lights

The indicator lights on the front of an external modem tell you what's happening during your communications session. The exact locations of the lights and the order in which they appear vary from modem to modem. But they are usually labeled with two-character abbreviations. Here's what the most common ones mean.

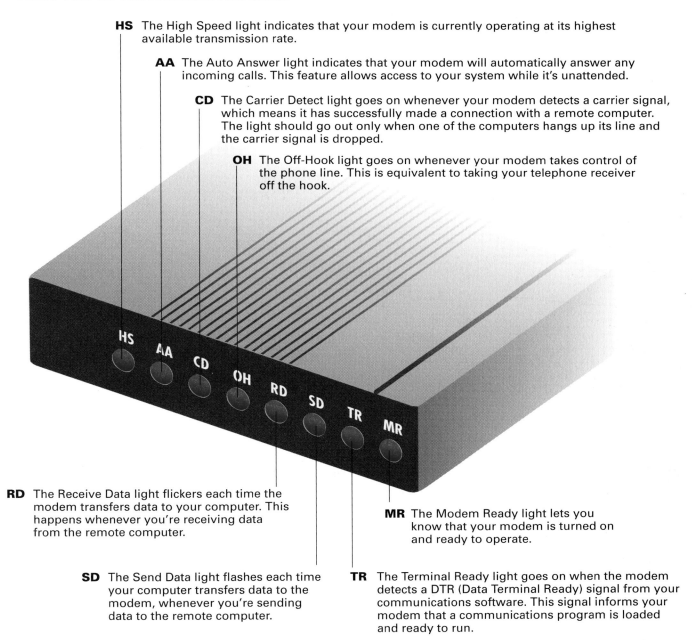

HS The High Speed light indicates that your modem is currently operating at its highest available transmission rate.

AA The Auto Answer light indicates that your modem will automatically answer any incoming calls. This feature allows access to your system while it's unattended.

CD The Carrier Detect light goes on whenever your modem detects a carrier signal, which means it has successfully made a connection with a remote computer. The light should go out only when one of the computers hangs up its line and the carrier signal is dropped.

OH The Off-Hook light goes on whenever your modem takes control of the phone line. This is equivalent to taking your telephone receiver off the hook.

RD The Receive Data light flickers each time the modem transfers data to your computer. This happens whenever you're receiving data from the remote computer.

SD The Send Data light flashes each time your computer transfers data to the modem, whenever you're sending data to the remote computer.

MR The Modem Ready light lets you know that your modem is turned on and ready to operate.

TR The Terminal Ready light goes on when the modem detects a DTR (Data Terminal Ready) signal from your communications software. This signal informs your modem that a communications program is loaded and ready to run.

CHAPTER 21

How a Scanner Works

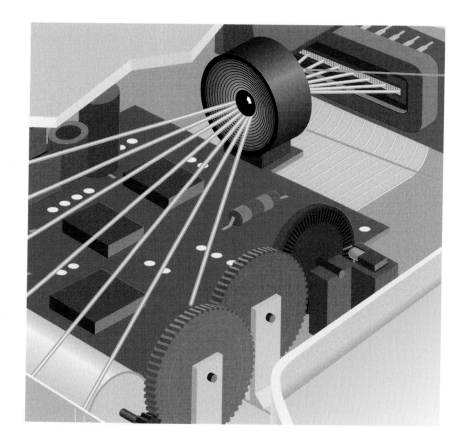

SCANNERS

SCANNERS are the eyes of your personal computer. They allow a PC to convert a drawing or photograph into code that a graphics or desktop publishing program can use to display the image on the screen, to reproduce the image with a graphics printer. Or a scanner can let you convert printed type into editable text with the help of optical character-recognition software.

The three basic types of scanners differ primarily in the way that the page containing the image and the scan head that reads the image move past each other. In a sheet-fed scanner, mechanical rollers move the paper past the scan head. In a flatbed scanner, the page is stationary behind a glass window while the head moves past the page, similar to the way a copying machine works. Hand-held scanners rely on the human hand to move the scan head.

Each method has its advantages and disadvantages. The flatbed scanner requires a series of mirrors to keep the image that is picked up by the moving scan head focused on the lens that feeds the image to a bank of sensors. Since no mirror is perfect, the image undergoes some degradation each time that it is reflected. But the advantage of a flatbed scanner is that it can scan oversized or thick documents, such as a book. With a sheet-fed scanner, the image is captured more accurately, but you're limited to scanning single, ordinary-sized sheets.

A hand-held scanner is a compromise. It can scan pages in books, but often the scanning head is not as wide as that in either a flatbed or a sheet-fed scanner. Most hand-scanner software automatically combines two half-page scans into a single image. The hand-held scanner, dependent on the steadiness of your hand to accurately render an image, is generally less expensive because it doesn't require a mechanism to move the scan head or paper.

A scanner's sophistication lies in its ability to translate an unlimited range of analog voltage levels into digital values. Some scanners can distinguish between only black and white, useful just for text or line art. More precise models can differentiate shades of gray. Color scanners use red, blue, and green filters to detect the colors in the reflected light.

Regardless of a scanner's sensitivity to gray or how the head and paper move, the operations of all scanners are basically simple and similar. We'll look at two that are representative of the technologies involved—a flatbed scanner and a hand-held grayscale scanner.

Flatbed Scanner

1 A light source illuminates a piece of paper placed face down against a glass window above the scanning mechanism. Blank or white spaces reflect more light than do inked or colored letters or images.

6 The digital information is sent to software in the PC, where the data is stored in a format with which a graphics program or an optical character-recognition program can work.

2 A motor moves the scan head beneath the page. As it moves, the scan head captures light bounced off individual areas of the page, each about 1/90,000 of an inch square.

3 The light from the page is reflected through a system of mirrors that must continually pivot to keep the light beams aligned with a lens.

4 A lens focuses the beams of light onto light-sensitive diodes that translate the amount of light into an electrical current. The more light that's reflected, the greater the voltage of the current.

5 An *analog-to-digital converter* (ADC) stores each analog reading of voltage as a digital pixel representing a black or white area along a line that contains 300 pixels to the inch. More sophisticated scanners can translate the voltages into shades of gray. If the scanner works with colored images, the scan head makes three passes under the images, and the light on each pass is directed through a red, green, or blue filter before it strikes the original image.

Hand-held Scanner

2 The lens focuses a single line of the image onto a *charge coupled device* (CCD), which is a component designed to detect subtle changes of voltage. The CCD contains a row of light detectors. As the light shines onto these detectors, each registers the amount of light as a voltage level that corresponds to white, black, gray, or to a color.

1 When you press the scan button on a typical hand-held scanner, a light-emitting diode (LED) illuminates the image beneath the scanner. An inverted, angled mirror directly above the scanner's window reflects the image onto a lens in the back of the scanner.

6 As the disk turns, a light shines through the slits and is detected by a photomicrosensor on the other side of the disk. Light striking the sensor throws a switch that sends a signal to the ADC. The signal tells the converter to send the line of bits generated by the converter to your PC. The converter clears itself of the data, and it is ready to receive a new stream of voltages from the next line of the image.

3 The voltages generated by the CCD are sent to a specialized analog chip for *gamma correction*, a process that enhances the black tones in an image so that the eye, which is more sensitive to dark tones than to light ones, will have an easier time recognizing the image. With some scanners, gamma correction is performed as a software process.

4 The single line of the image now passes to an analog-to-digital converter (ADC). In a grayscale scanner, the converter assigns 8 bits to each pixel, which translates into 256 levels of gray in the final digitized image. The ADC on a monochrome scanner registers only 1 bit per pixel, either on or off, representing, respectively, black or white.

5 As your hand moves the scanner, a hard rubber roller—the main purpose of which is to keep the scanner's path straight—also turns a series of gears that rotate a slotted disk.

CHAPTER
22

How a Digital Camera Works

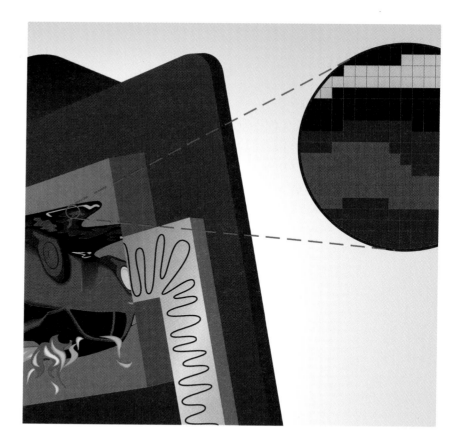

PREDICTION:

By the year 2000, the old camera that you used to stuff film in will be retired to the back of some closet. In its place will be a digital camera, one that uses light-sensitive electronics instead of film to capture images. Instead of a photo album, you'll store your pictures of the kids and that vacation to the Grand Canyon on your PC's hard drive or a writable CD-ROM (see Chapter 24).

Digital photography is not new, although most digitized photos have made their way to disk via conventional photography and a scanner. Digital cameras that eliminate the scanner as middleman already exist. The best of them, however, range in cost from expensive to ridiculous. But the technology is no mystery, and all any of the cameras need to do to significantly replace film cameras is to improve resolution a bit and come down in price. The change will be a revolution in how we visually capture memories and document life.

The step from film to electronics shouldn't be surprising. Both have a lot in common. For example, a good photograph appears to be one smooth, seamless image of widely varying color, darkness, and contrast. If you examine it closely enough, you will see that it chemically consists of the same elements found in electronic photography. Color film is made up of thin layers of chemicals that react to three different colors, just as PC displays are made of three colors. And chemical film has its own equivalent of a screen's pixels. The film uses the grains of silver compounds that react to light by clumping together to create tiny dots of black and white or different colors. The more and smaller the clumps, the finer the film's resolution. On fine-grained film the naked eye can't see the clumps. But with a film that sacrifices resolution for light sensitivity, a close look will reveal the photo's graininess; you're able to see dots of black and color that unresolve into a mosaic of the image. For most 35mm film there are about 2 million clumps of silver that make up the image. The best digital cameras come close with 1.5 million pixels, each capable of registering whether it has been struck by light. Most digital cameras under $1,000, with resolutions of about 180,000 pixels and simple optics, are more toys than professional tools.

There's a great deal of variety in how digital cameras store the visual data once the shutter is snapped. The image can be stored in RAM, to the camera's own hard or floppy drives, to a PC Card, or through a direct connection to a desktop PC. Eventually, of course, all digital photos wind up on a PC's hard disk. There, the images can be manipulated, which is the digital equivalent of darkroom retouching. The images are then displayed or printed.

The manipulation of digital photographs is a distinct jump from chemical photography, where retouching is a difficult job best left to a professional. Image editing software, such as Adobe Photoshop or Painter, makes it possible for an amateur to morph photos of a husband and wife to take a stab at how their children might look or for someone to neatly delete a divorced spouse from a family photo.

Digital Cameras

2 Instead of being focused on photographic film, the image is focused on a chip called a *charge coupled device* (CCD). The face of the CCD is studded with an array of transistors that create electrical currents in proportion to the intensity of the light striking them. The transistors make up the pixels of the image. On a PC's screen or in an input device, such as scanner or a digital camera, a pixel is the minimum, distinct visual information a component can display or capture. The pixel may be made up of only one transistor for black-and-white photography, or several transistors for color. The more pixels in an image, the better its resolution.

1 Light passes through the lens of a digital camera the same as it does in a film camera.

3 The transistors generate a continuous, analog electrical signal that goes to an analog-to-digital converter (ADC). The ADC is a chip that translates the varying signal to a digital format, which consists of a continuous stream of 1s and 0s.

4 The ADC sends the digital information to a digital signal processor (DSP) that has been programmed specifically to manipulate photographic images. The DSP adjusts the contrast and detail in the image, compresses the data that makes up the image so it takes up less storage space, and sends the data to the camera's storage medium.

5 The image is temporarily stored on a hard drive or in RAM built into the camera body, and from there it's transferred to a PC's permanent storage through a serial or SCSI cable. Or, the image may be saved to a special mini-floppy drive or a PC Card plugged into the camera. Being portable types of storage, the floppy or PC Card can be removed from the camera and inserted into a matching connection on a PC, where it's copied to a hard drive or writable CD-ROM. Some cameras that create files of 20MB or larger may be cabled to a PC while a photo is being shot, instantly transmitting the image directly to the computer.

C H A P T E R

23

How a PC Card (PCMCIA) Works

BARELY bigger than a credit card, the PC Card is a miracle of microcomputing miniaturization. These cards can contain anything from a modem or network adapter to a solid-state hard disk. They're all packed into a tiny package and made to work with your portable PC, increasing the versatility of portables while increasing their weight by only an ounce or so. Plug in one card and your notebook has a built-in new modem. Plug in another and it's got a SCSI connection for a hard drive or CD-ROM drive.

The most common place to find a slot for a PC Card is on a portable computer, naturally. But they're not limited to pint-sized PCs. A PC Card slot on a notebook and another on a desktop mean you can use the same PC Card on either. The advantage: When you take a trip, you can slip that hard drive PC Card out of your desktop PC and into your portable. You take all your work with you without the hassle of feeding floppies into both computers or running a file-transfer cable between their parallel ports.

Originally, PC Cards were called PCMCIA cards, one of the more unlovely of computer acronyms. It was supposed to stand for Personal Computer Memory Card Interface Association, but others thought of a different meaning for it: People Can't Master Computer Industry Acronyms. It's a shame the device began life with such a terrible name, and truthfully "PC Card" isn't much better because it sounds too much like expansion card.

But name snafus aside, PC Cards are terrific inventions because one of the ultimate goals of computing is to make the buggers so tiny and lightweight that they'll be like Dick Tracy's wrist radio. *Digital signal processing*—which lets the same device process different kinds of communications—may in the future allow a single card to function as different types of devices. We've still got a way to go to witness those miracles, but the important thing to remember right now is that if you're buying a portable computer, make sure it has at least one PC Card slot—two are even better. There are different types of slots; some are made to accommodate a slightly thicker card. Before buying any PC Card notebook, check out what cards are available for the type of slot the computer is sporting.

PC Cards

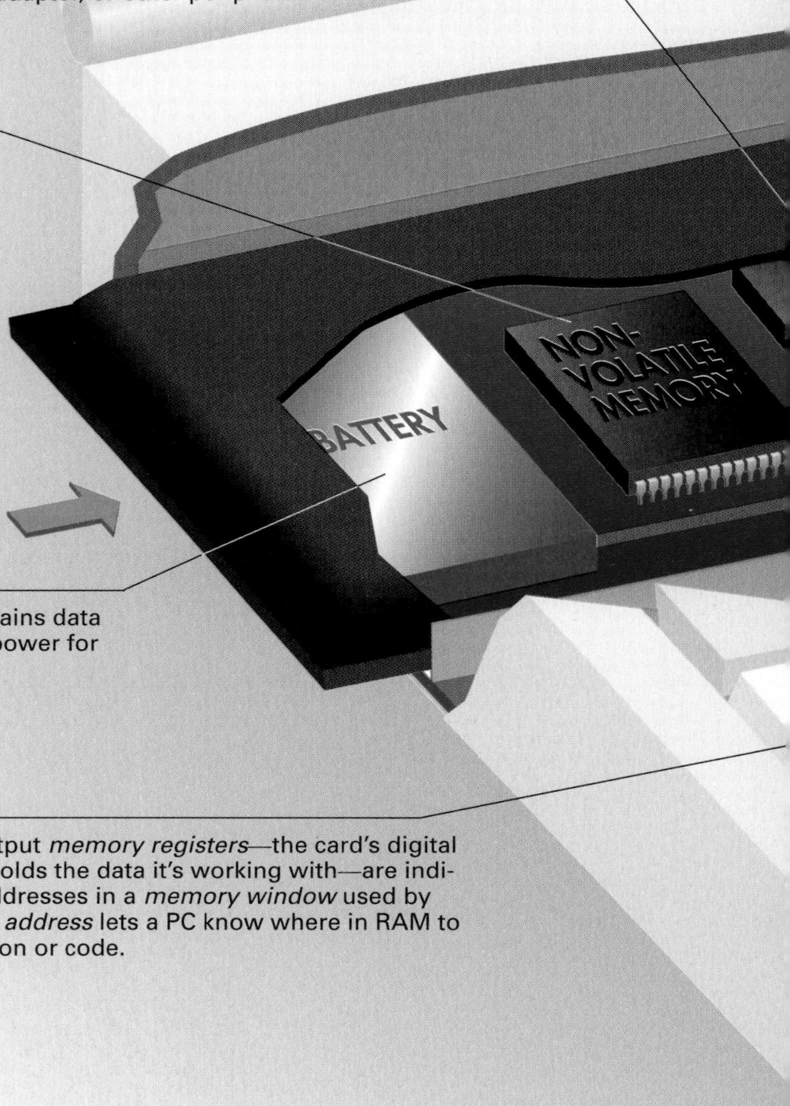

1 At the factory, most of the circuity in the PC Card may be installed in the form of RAM, in which case the card is designed for use as a solid-state drive, such as the one shown here. Some PC Cards actually contain a real, spinning hard drive. Alternatively, the circuitry may function as a modem, network adapter, SCSI adapter, or other peripheral.

2 In *non-volatile memory*—which doesn't lose its contents when power is turned off—the PC Card stores configuration information about itself so that no jumpers or DIP switches need to be changed to set it up. This information determines how the laptop accesses the card. The data is coordinated with a *device driver* that's run on the laptop during boot-up so the portable PC can have access to the card. A device driver is a software extension to the operating system that lets DOS or Windows know how to communicate with a specific piece of hardware.

3 A battery built into the card maintains data stored in any RAM and provides power for the card to work.

4 Memory and input/output *memory registers*—the card's digital scratch pad where it holds the data it's working with—are individually mapped to addresses in a *memory window* used by the laptop. A *memory address* lets a PC know where in RAM to store or find information or code.

NON-VOLATILE MEMORY

BATTERY

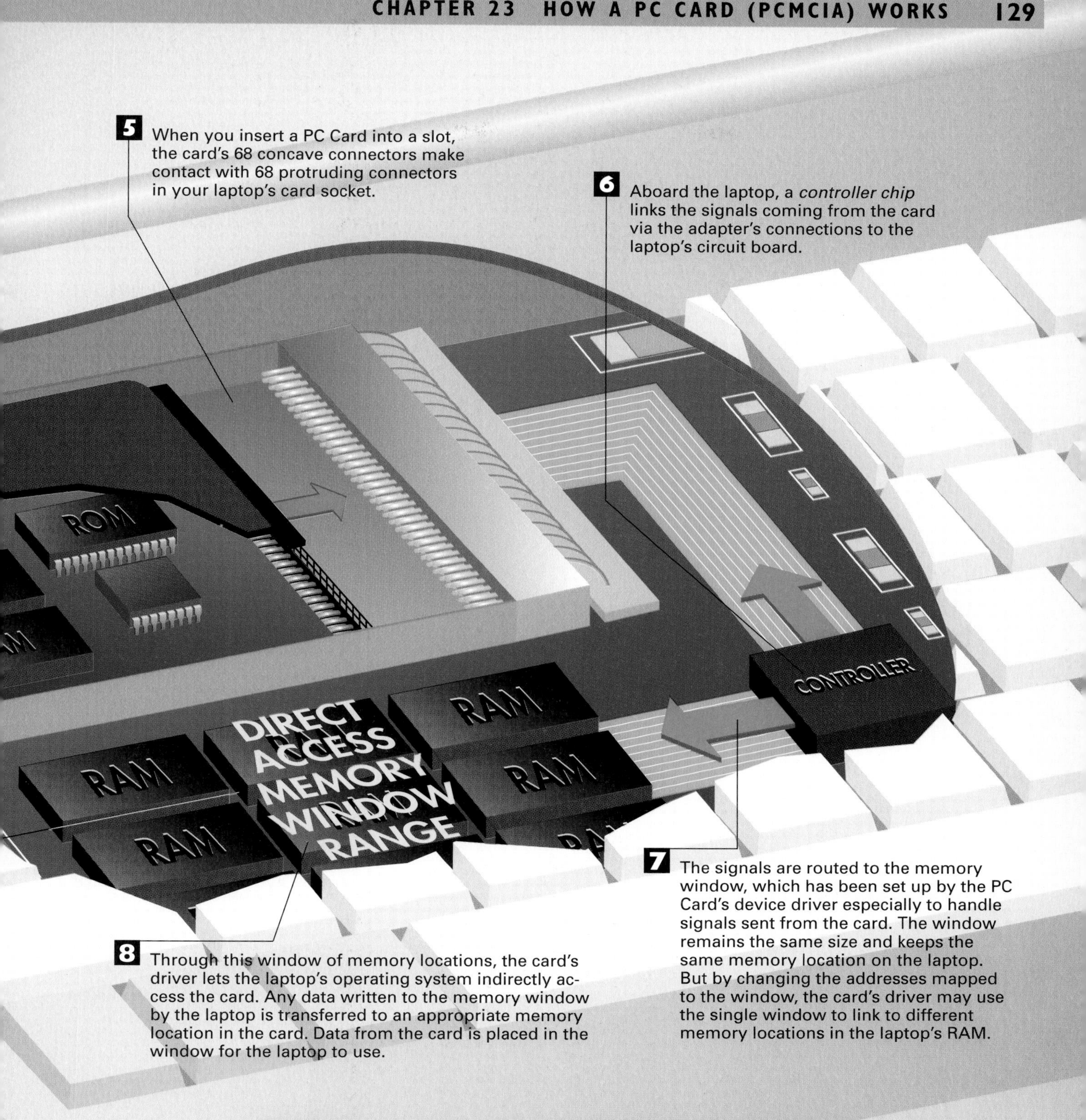

5 When you insert a PC Card into a slot, the card's 68 concave connectors make contact with 68 protruding connectors in your laptop's card socket.

6 Aboard the laptop, a *controller chip* links the signals coming from the card via the adapter's connections to the laptop's circuit board.

ROM

DIRECT ACCESS MEMORY WINDOW RANGE

RAM

RAM

RAM

RAM

CONTROLLER

7 The signals are routed to the memory window, which has been set up by the PC Card's device driver especially to handle signals sent from the card. The window remains the same size and keeps the same memory location on the laptop. But by changing the addresses mapped to the window, the card's driver may use the single window to link to different memory locations in the laptop's RAM.

8 Through this window of memory locations, the card's driver lets the laptop's operating system indirectly access the card. Any data written to the memory window by the laptop is transferred to an appropriate memory location in the card. Data from the card is placed in the window for the laptop to use.

NOTE Theoretically, systems that support the PC Card standard can have up to 255 adapter plugs, each capable of connecting to as many as 16 card sockets. That means, hypothetically, a single system could have up to 4,080 PC Cards attached to it.

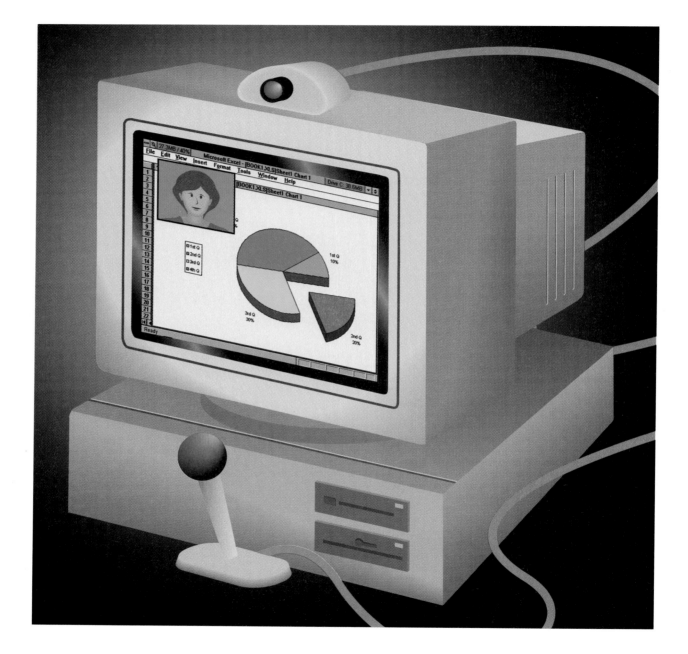

P A R T

MULTIMEDIA

THE original IBM PC, compared to today's personal computers, was a poor, introverted little thing. It didn't speak, it didn't sing or play the guitar. It didn't even display graphics well or show more than four colors at a time. Not only is today's multimedia revolution changing the ways we use PCs, but also our use of information itself. Where information was formerly defined as columns of numbers or pages of text, we're communicating—both to and from—our PCs, using our voices, our ears, and our eyes, not simply to read, but to see pure visuals.

What makes a PC a multimedia PC? It's easy to identify multimedia with a CD-ROM drive, which plays computer discs that look like the compact discs played on audio CD players. But a CD-ROM drive in itself does not multimedia make. The first CDs were collections of text—dictionaries, all of Shakespeare's works, adaptations of self-help books—with at best a spare graphic or two. They were not what we think of as multimedia today because they did not have sound or video. In addition to a CD-ROM drive, a multimedia PC must have a sound card, speakers, and the hardware and software needed to display videos and animations. There are, in fact, industry standards for what types of hardware make up an official multimedia PC.

The Multimedia PC 2 (MPC 2) standard specifies how fast a CD-ROM must transfer data to the CPU, how much detail is in the sounds played and recorded by the sound board, and the processor power needed to handle sound and video. In case you're wondering, yes, there is an older MPC 1 standard. And there will probably be an MPC 3. And without getting into the details of any of them, the important thing to know when shopping is to look for an MPC 2 sticker on computers and multimedia components to make sure you get hardware that's up to par. There are faster CD-ROM drives, faster video cards that produce bigger video images, and sound subsystems that capture and create richer, more realistic sounds. But at least make sure the multimedia PC you get meets the minimum requirements of the current MPC standard.

To reproduce multimedia outside of Windows, you should have programs and drivers that came with your sound card, and some DOS games supply their own programs to play sounds and video. If you have Windows, you have all the software you need to run multimedia. To record video with sound, most multimedia CDs use either Microsoft's Video for Windows or Apple's QuickTime. Windows' Media Player can replay videos from these and other sources, along with digitized sound, and audio CDs.

Put together all these features—voices, music, video, animations—and what do you get? Television! But television in a screen that's only about 3 × 4 inches—although it weighs

40 pounds. As television, it'd be laughed out of any self-respecting electronics boutique. As captivating as video and sound are, concentrating on them as elements of multimedia overlooks what makes TV, movies, or music into multimedia: access.

A CD-ROM is a random access device, the same as memory, hard drives, and floppy drives. They can all access any one piece of data they contain as easily as they can any other data. By contrast, a videotape, movie on film, and tape recordings are sequential access devices. You can't get to data at the end of that sequential information —whether it's the airport scene in *Casablanca* or the last track of a Pink Floyd cassette tape—unless you first go past every other piece of information embedded on the tape or film. You can fast-forward, but there's still a big difference in the time it takes to access the first piece of information and the last. But with a movie on CD-ROM, such as *It's a Wonderful Life* or *A Hard Day's Night,* you can skip directly to any scene you like. There's a slight delay, but it doesn't differ that much whether you're going to a scene at the start, middle or end of the movie. That's the real advantage to multimedia CDs— sound and visuals combined with text and easy, quick access.

CHAPTER

24

How a CD-ROM Drive Works

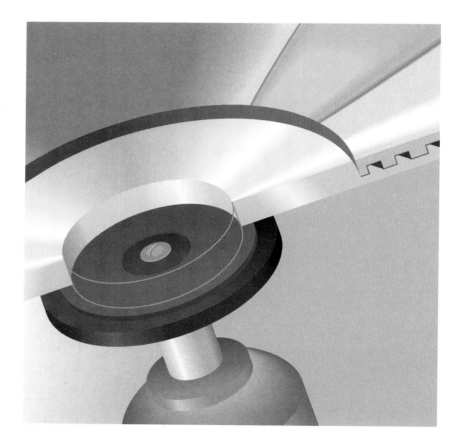

A computer's CD-ROM drive uses small, interchangeable, plastic-encased discs from which data is retrieved using a laser beam, much like compact music discs. And like a music CD, a computer CD-ROM stores vast amounts of information. This is achieved by using light to record data in a form that's more tightly packed than the relatively clumsy magnetic read/write heads a conventional drive must manage. And like music CD players, computer CD-ROM drives are appearing in jukebox configurations that automatically change among six to 100 CDs as you request different information.

Unlike an audio CD player, however, a CD-ROM drive is nearly devoid of buttons and LCD readouts, except for a button to load and unload a disc and few lights to tell you when the drive is reading a disc or playing music. The drive is controlled by software in your PC that sends instructions to controller circuitry that's either a part of the computer's motherboard or on a separate board installed in an expansion slot. Together, the software and circuitry manipulate high-tech components that make conventional drives seem crude in comparison.

The CD-ROMs that are most common are, again like music compact discs, read-only. Your PC can't write your own data or files to these discs; your PC can only retrieve the information that was stamped on the CDs at the factory. The huge capacity and read-only nature of most CD-ROMs, combined with the relatively low cost of the drives, makes the discs the perfect medium for storing reams of data that doesn't need updating. You can easily find CD-ROMs filled with clip art, photographs, encyclopedias, the complete works of Shakespeare and entire bookshelves of reference material. CD-ROM drives are also a basic component of multimedia systems, which use video and sound files that need the voluminous storage CDs supply. (An added bonus of their multimedia capabilities is that most CD-ROM drives will also let you play ordinary stereo music discs.)

And lately CD drives have been getting into the writing business. The price has been falling for CD-R (CD-Recordable) drives that can write data to a special type of compact disc. There are, however, still two catches that prevent CD drives from totally displacing hard drives. One catch is that CD drives are still slow. A drive that meets the Multimedia PC 2 standard for performance only has to move 300 kilobytes of data a second. A good hard drive, by comparison, transfers 10,000 kilobytes a second. The other catch is that you can't write to portions of a writable CD-ROM that already have data written to them. You can add to data that was written to the disc in an earlier session but you can't delete or change what's already there. Still, writable CD drives have a strong future for both in-house and professional multimedia development, as well as for archiving data.

CD-ROM Drive

6 Each pulse of light that strikes the light-sensing diode generates a small electrical voltage. These voltages are matched against a timing circuit to generate a stream of 1s and 0s that the computer can understand.

5 Light that strikes a pit is scattered, but light that strikes a land is reflected directly back at the detector, where it passes through a prism that deflects the reflected laser beam to a light-sensing diode.

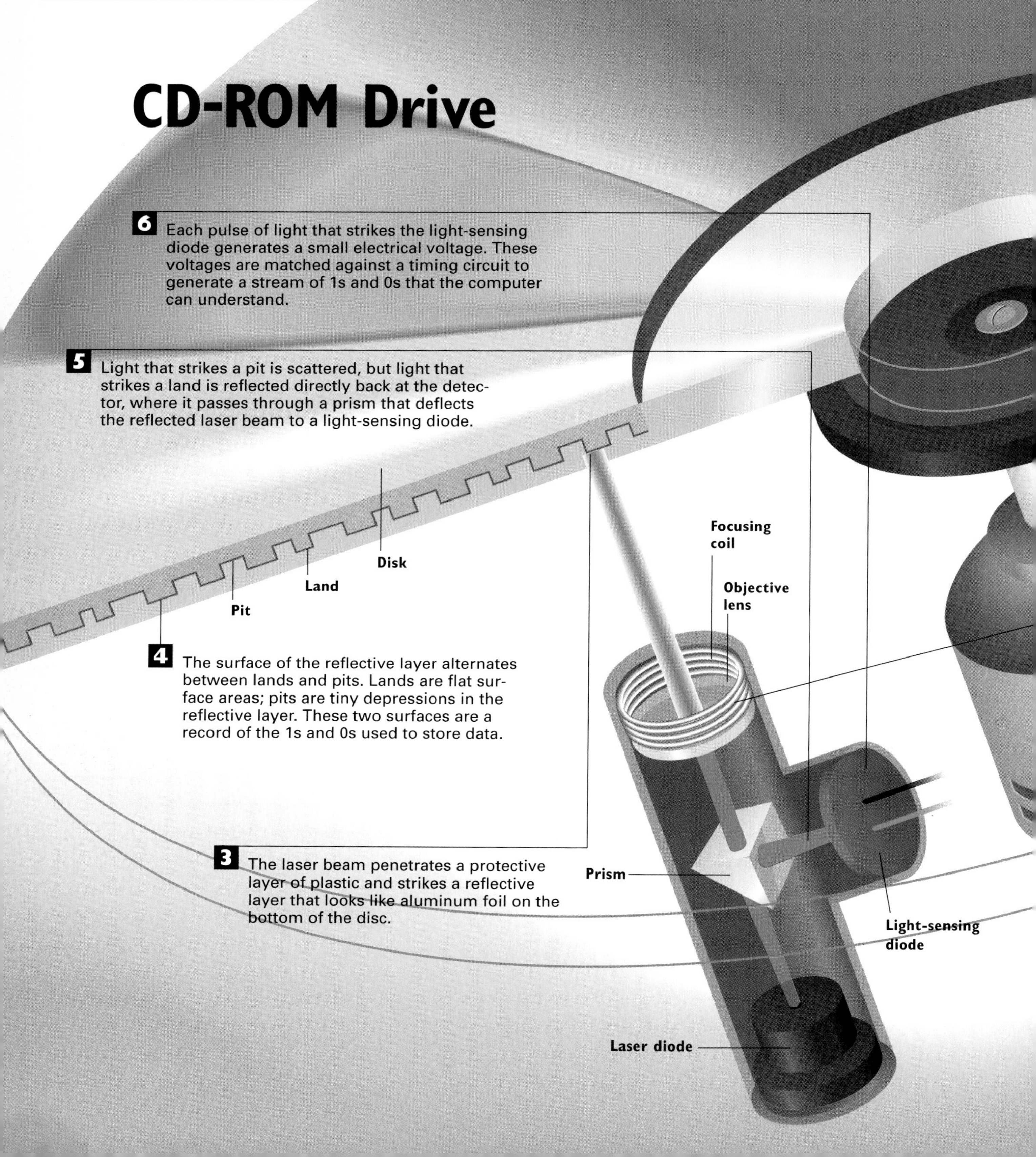

Disk

Land

Pit

Focusing coil

Objective lens

4 The surface of the reflective layer alternates between lands and pits. Lands are flat surface areas; pits are tiny depressions in the reflective layer. These two surfaces are a record of the 1s and 0s used to store data.

Prism

3 The laser beam penetrates a protective layer of plastic and strikes a reflective layer that looks like aluminum foil on the bottom of the disc.

Light-sensing diode

Laser diode

1 A motor constantly varies the rate at which a CD-ROM disc spins so that regardless of where a component, called a detector, is located in relation to the radius of the disk, the portion of the disc immediately above the detector is always moving at the same speed. (See Notes below.)

2 The laser projects a concentrated beam of light that is further focused by a focusing coil.

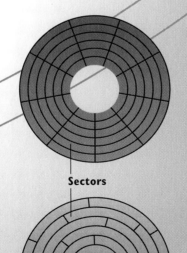

Sectors

NOTE Magnetic disks such as those used in hard drives have data arranged in concentric circles called tracks, which are divided radially into sectors. Using a scheme called *constant angular velocity*, the magnetic disk always spins at the same rate; that is, the tracks near the periphery of the disk are moving faster than the tracks near the center. Because the outside sectors are moving past the read\write heads faster, the sectors must be physically larger to hold the same amount of data as the inner sectors. This format wastes a great deal of storage space but maximizes the speed with which data can be retrieved.

NOTE Typically, CD-ROM discs use a different scheme than do magnetic disks to stake out the areas of the disc where data is recorded. Instead of several tracks arranged in concentric circles, on the CD-ROM disc, data is contained in a single track that spirals from the center of the disc to its circumference. The track is still divided by sectors, but each sector is the same physical size. Using a method called *constant linear velocity*, the disc drive constantly varies the rate at which the disc is spinning so that as the detector moves toward the center of the disc, the disc speeds up. The effect is that a compact disc can contain more sectors than a magnetic disk and, therefore, more data.

Writable CD-ROM

1 A laser sends a low-energy light beam at a compact disc built on a relatively thick layer of clear polycarbonate plastic. On top of the plastic is a layer of dyed color material that is usually green, a thin layer of gold to reflect the laser beam, a protective layer of lacquer, and often a layer of scratch-resistant polymer material. There may be a paper or silk-screened label on top of all that.

2 The laser's write head follows a tight spiral groove cut into the plastic layer. The groove, called an *atip* (absolute timing in pregroove), has a continuous wave pattern similar to that on a phonograph record. The frequency of the waves varies continuously from the start of the groove to its end. The laser beam reflects off the wave pattern, and by reading the frequency of the waves, the CD drive can calculate where the head is located in relation to the surface of the disc.

3 As the head follows the atip, it uses the position information provided by the groove's waves to control the speed of the motor turning the disc so that the area of the disc under the head is always moving at the same speed. To do this, this disc must spin faster as the head moves toward the center of the disc and slower as the head approaches the rim.

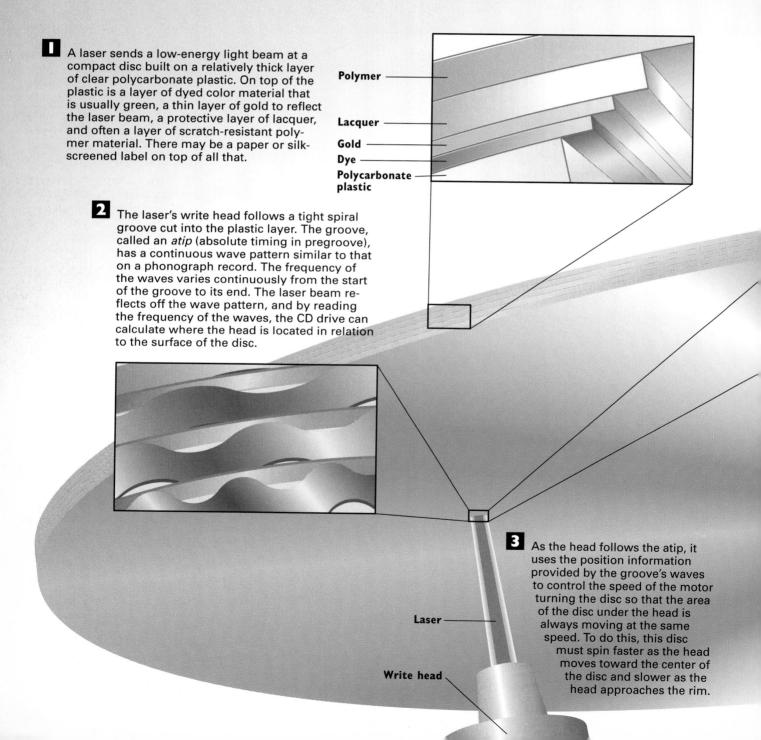

Polymer

Lacquer

Gold

Dye

Polycarbonate plastic

Laser

Write head

5 The dye layer is designed to absorb light at that specific frequency. Absorbing the energy from the laser beam creates a mark in one of three ways, depending on the design of the disc. The dye may be bleached; the polycarbonate layer may be distorted; or the dye layer may form a bubble. Regardless of how the mark is created, the result is a distortion called a *stripe* along the spiral track. When the beam is switched off, no mark appears. The lengths of the stripes vary, as do the unmarked spaces among them. The CD drive uses the varying lengths to write the information in a special code that compresses the data and checks for errors. The change in the dye is permanent, making the recordable compact disc a write-once, read-many (WORM) medium.

6 The CD-recordable drive—or an ordinary read-only CD drive—focuses a lower-powered laser beam onto the disc to read data. Where a mark has not been made on the surface of the disc, the gold layer reflects the beam straight back to the read head. When the beam hits a stripe, the distortion in the groove scatters the beam so that the light is not returned to the read head. The results are the same as if the beam were aimed at the lands and pits in an ordinary CD-ROM. Each time the beam is reflected to the head, the head generates a pulse of electricity. From the pattern in the pulses of current, the drive decompresses the data, error-checks it, and passes it along to the PC in the digital form of 0s and 1s.

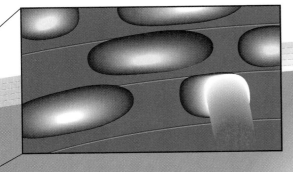

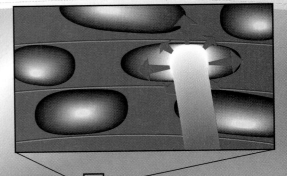

4 The software used to make a compact disc recording sends the data to be stored to the CD in a specific format, such as *ISO 9096*, which automatically corrects errors and creates a table of contents. The table is needed because there is nothing like the *file allocation table* on a magnetic disk to keep track of a file's location. The CD drive records the information by sending a higher-powered pulse of the laser beam at a light frequency of 780 nanometers.

Read head

CD Jukebox

2 CDs are stored in cassettes that each hold a half-dozen discs. Each disc rests in a thin plastic tray that's open on the top.

1 A CD drive such as the Pioneer DRM-1804X uses a jukebox mechanism to automate putting any of up to 18 CD-ROMs in position for the read head to retrieve their data when the PC user changes to a different CD-ROM drive letter. Other multidisk drives—more elaborate, expensive, and the size of a refrigerator—can retrieve discs from as many as 100 CDs or more.

3 When the PC sends a signal to the drive to load a CD, gears turn to raise or lower the jukebox's read head mechanism until it's at a height matching that of the CD the computer has asked for.

4 When the drive is on the right level, the drive stops the read head and another motor swings out the tray holding the CD and moves it into the head mechanism

5 The head clamps onto the disc, raises it so that the disc is free of the tray, and the head's spindle motor spins the disc. The read head's laser moves along the disc's groove, reading data from the reflections off the disc.

6 When the PC requests a different disc, the head mechanism lets go of the disc that's already loaded and places it back into the tray, which returns the disc to the cassette. Then the head mechanism moves to the level of the new CD. It takes about 10 seconds to unload one CD and begin reading from another.

CHAPTER

25

How Multimedia Sound Works

FOR years DOS and Windows personal computers sounded like a cartoon roadrunner. They could play only loud, high-pitched beeps and low-pitched beeps. But they were still only beeps. There was no hiding that fact.

We owe today's multimedia sound abilities to game players. They saw the advantages of hearing realistic explosions, rocket blasts, gun shots, and mood-setting background music long before developers creating business software realized the practical advantages of sound. Now, you can listen to your PC speak instructions as you follow along on the keyboard, dictate a letter by talking into your PC, give your PC spoken commands, attach a voice message to a document, and not have to take your eyes off a hard-copy list while your PC sounds out the numbers as you're typing them into a spreadsheet.

None of the multimedia that enhances business, personal, and family use of a PC could exist without sound capabilities. Multimedia CD-ROMs bring their subject to life in ways not possible in books because you hear the actual sounds of whales, wars, and warblers, of sopranos, space shots, and saxophones. Not that sound capabilities must always enlighten you on a topic. You should have fun with your PC, too. It won't make the day shorter to replace Windows' error chime with Homer Simpson saying, "Doh!" And you won't be more productive every time a Windows program opens or closes if it makes a sound like those doors in *Star Trek*. But so what? Taking advantage of the sounds in a multimedia PC adds to the fun of using your computer. And we all spend too much time in front of these things for it not to be fun.

Sound has become so important that it's helped lead to the development of a chip called a *digital signal processor* (DSP) that relieves the computer's main CPU of most of the processing chores involving sound. Eventually, expect to find other types of digital signals, such as voice mail, fax, and video managed by a single DSP that simply follows different instructions for the different types of signals. And now that the PC has a voice, it's become fluent in many different digital languages. We'll look at some of them in this chapter, and how your PC's sound card translates digital records of voices, music, and sound into vibrating reality.

Multimedia Sound

Digital Signal Processing

1 From microphones or other equipment such as an audio CD player, a sound card receives a sound in its native format, a continuous analog signal of a sound wave that contains frequencies and volumes that are constantly changing. The sound card can handle more than one signal at a time, allowing you to record sounds in stereo.

2 The signals go to an analog-to-digital converter (ADC) chip. The chip changes the continuous analog signal into the 0s and 1s of digital data.

3 A ROM chip contains the instructions for handling the digital signal. Newer designs use an EPROM (erasable, programmable read only memory) chip instead of ROM. The EPROM chip allows the board to be updated with improved instructions as they're developed.

4 The ADC sends the binary information to a chip called a *digital signal processor* (DSP) that relieves the computer's main CPU of most of the processing chores involving sound. The DSP gets its instructions about what to do with that data from the ROM chip. Typically, the DSP compresses the incoming signal so that it takes less storage space.

5 The DSP sends the compressed data to the PC's main processor, which, in turn, sends the data to a hard drive to be stored.

6 To play a recorded sound, the CPU fetches the file containing the compressed, digital replication of the sound from a hard drive or CD-ROM and sends the data to the DSP.

7 The DSP decompresses the data on the fly, and sends it to a digital-to-audio converter (DAC) chip, which translates the digital information to a constantly wavering electrical current.

8 The analog current is amplified, usually by an amplifier built into the PC's speakers. Then the stronger current powers an electromagnet that's part of the speaker, causing the speaker's *cone* to vibrate, creating sound.

Wave Table versus FM Synthesis

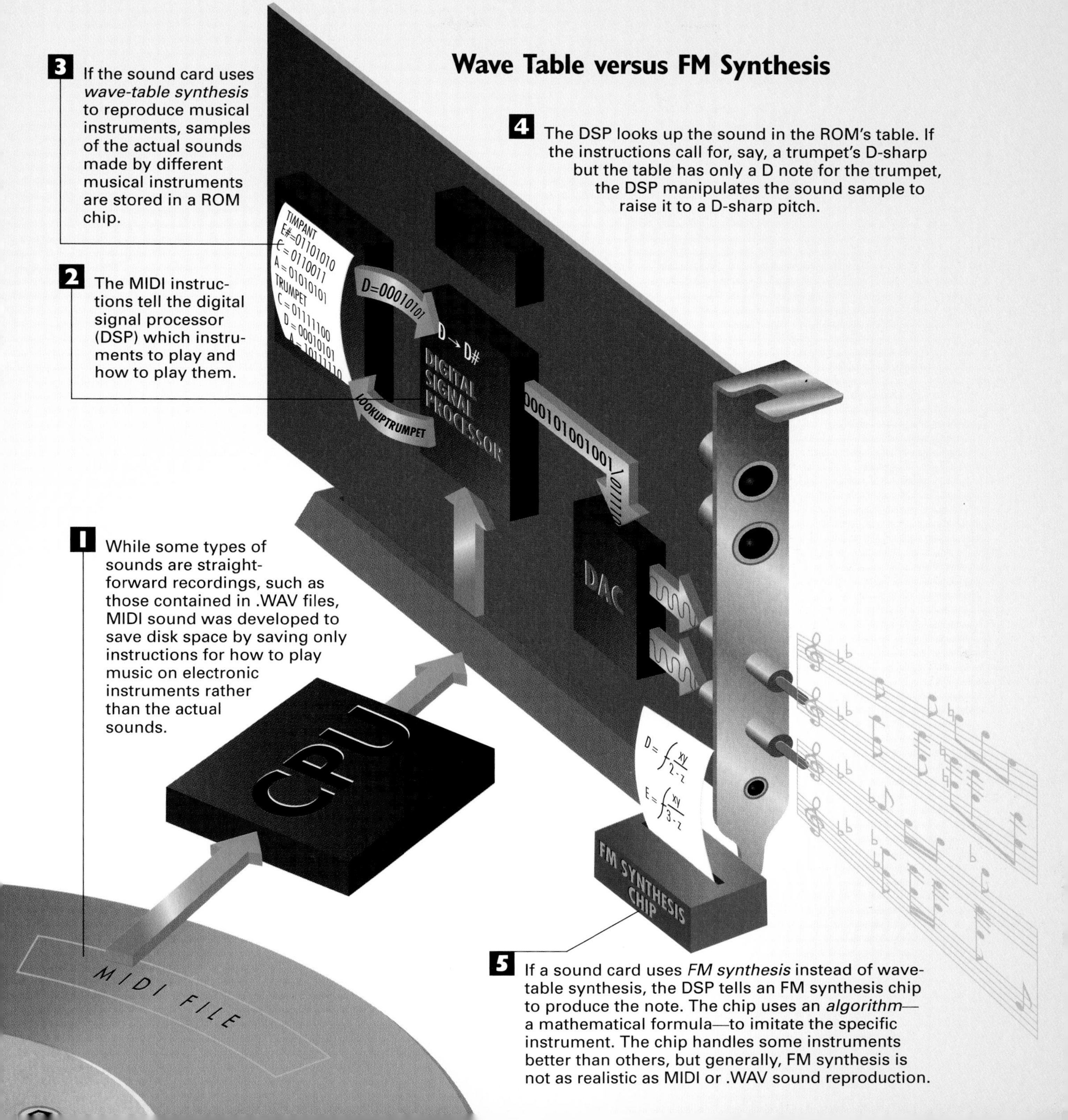

3 If the sound card uses *wave-table synthesis* to reproduce musical instruments, samples of the actual sounds made by different musical instruments are stored in a ROM chip.

2 The MIDI instructions tell the digital signal processor (DSP) which instruments to play and how to play them.

4 The DSP looks up the sound in the ROM's table. If the instructions call for, say, a trumpet's D-sharp but the table has only a D note for the trumpet, the DSP manipulates the sound sample to raise it to a D-sharp pitch.

TIMPANT
E#=01101010
C = 0110011
A = 01010101
TRUMPET
C = 01111100
D = 00010101
A = 10111110

D=00010101

D → D#

LOOKUP TRUMPET

DIGITAL SIGNAL PROCESSOR

00010100100111011

DAC

1 While some types of sounds are straight-forward recordings, such as those contained in .WAV files, MIDI sound was developed to save disk space by saving only instructions for how to play music on electronic instruments rather than the actual sounds.

CPU

$$D = \int \frac{xy}{2-2}$$

$$E = \int \frac{xy}{3-2}$$

FM SYNTHESIS CHIP

MIDI FILE

5 If a sound card uses *FM synthesis* instead of wave-table synthesis, the DSP tells an FM synthesis chip to produce the note. The chip uses an *algorithm*— a mathematical formula—to imitate the specific instrument. The chip handles some instruments better than others, but generally, FM synthesis is not as realistic as MIDI or .WAV sound reproduction.

CHAPTER
26 How Multimedia Video Works

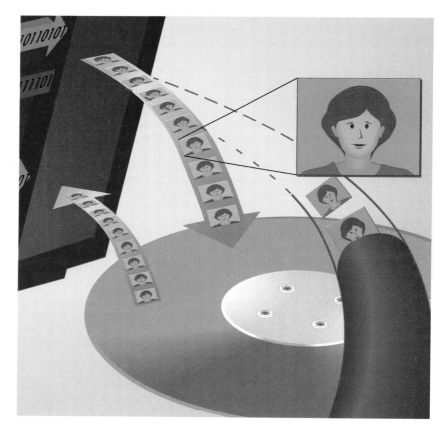

VIDEO

VIDEO is nothing new. We grew up with Howdy Doody, Gilligan, and "Cheers." The camcorder is replacing the 35mm still camera as the memory-catcher of choice. So why does video's arrival on PCs seem like such news? It's precisely because we are just that used to relying on talking, moving pictures to get so much of the information we need to conduct business and our personal lives.

All the excitement and technical innovations in multimedia concentrate on video and audio, which has it all backwards. The excitement isn't really in what video brings to computers. It's what computers bring to video. Although multimedia audio rivals a good home stereo system, video on PCs is still sadly lacking. You must usually make do with a video window about a tenth of the overall size of your PC's screen. The video is likely to be jerky, and the words and lip movements match each other only randomly. The truth is you get better video from a home-made tape on slow play.

So why not just use videotape to convey information? Because videotape doesn't have *random access.* The freedom to move to any point is random access. It's where RAM gets its name, *random access memory.* Early computers used magnetic tapes to store programs and data, and using them was slow. Random access memory and random access hard drives give computers their speed and versatility.

And it's exactly this issue of access that differentiates multimedia video from a videotape. You have control over what you see and hear. Instead of following a preprogrammed course of videos and animation, you can skip about as you like, accessing those parts of a multimedia program that interest you most. Or with videoconferencing, you can interact live with another person in a different part of the world and work on the same document or graphic simultaneously.

Despite the superficial resemblance between a TV set and a PC monitor, the two produce an image in different ways. The TV is an analog device that gets its information from continuously varying broadcasting waves. A computer's monitor uses analog current to control the image, but the data for what to display comes from digital information—0s and 1s.

The flood of data can easily exceed what a display can handle. That's why multimedia video is so small and looks so jerky. A smaller image means less information—literally, fewer pixels—the PC has to track and update. The jerkiness comes from the fact that the image is updated only five to 15 times a second, compared to 30 frames for a TV or movie. By further increasing data compression, some of these limitations have been almost eliminated. MPEG compression, for example, lets multimedia video cover the entire screen. Further development of the techniques described here for compressing and transmitting will eventually make computer video as ubiquitous as sitcom reruns.

Multimedia Video

1 A camera and microphone capture the picture and sounds of a video and send analog signals to a video-capture adapter board. To cut down on the amount of data that must be processed, the board captures only about half the number of frames per second that movies use.

8 Videoconferencing also uses *lossy* compression. Within each frame, differences that are unnoticeable or nearly so are discarded. A slight variation in the background here, for example, is sacrificed so that the system will not have to handle the information needed to display that difference.

7 MPEG (Motion Pictures Expert Group) compression, which is effective enough to produce full-screen video, only records key frames and then predicts what the missing frames look like by comparing the changes in the key frames.

6 Advanced forms of compressing both recorded video and videoconferencing use a sampling process to cut down on the amount of data that must be recorded or transmitted. One method, used by .AVI, makes a record of one complete video frame, and then records only the differences—the delta—in the frames that follow. Each frame is re-created by combining the delta data with the data for the frame that preceded it.

2 On the video capture adapter card, an analog-to-digital converter (ADC) chip converts the wavering analog video and audio signals to a pattern of 0s and 1s, the binary language that describes all computer data.

3 A compression/decompression chip or software reduces the amount of data needed to re-create the video signals. As an example, the software compression for Microsoft Video for Windows looks for redundant information. Here, the background is a large expanse of a single color—blue. Rather than save the same information for each pixel that makes up the background, compression saves the color data for that exact shade of blue only once, along with directions for where to use the color when the video is replayed.

4 Video for Windows saves more space when it writes the video to disk by interweaving with each other the data for the picture and audio in a file format called .AVI for audio/video interleave. To replay the video, the compressed and combined video and audio data is either sent through a compression/decompression chip or processed by software. Either method restores areas that had been eliminated by compression. The combined audio and video elements of the signal are separated and both are sent to a digital-to-analog converter (DAC), which translates that binary data into analog signals that go to the screen and speakers.

5 Instead of being recorded, the compressed video and audio signals may be sent over special telephone lines, such as ISDN (integrated services digital network), that transmit the data in a digital form rather than as the analog signal used by ordinary phone lines. A similarly equipped PC at a remote location receives the digital signals, decompresses them, and converts them to the analog signals needed to control the display and audio playback.

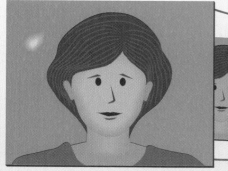

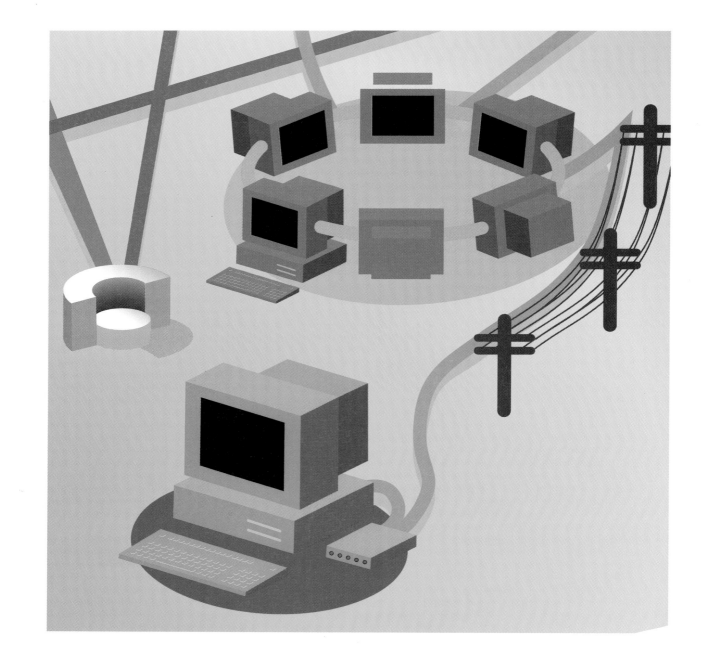

P A R T

6

NETWORKS

BEFORE

the emergence of the PC, there was the terminal—a rather dumb display—and a keyboard; these gave computer users at the same location access to the same centralized computer. Usually, that computer was a large, mysterious box off in some other room, where it was tended by specialists in white lab coats.

The system was not unlike some primitive religions in which the high priests were the only ones with the secret knowledge of how to communicate with their god. Mere users were forbidden to enter the temple and certainly could not address the computer god directly. The people sitting in front of the terminal had to be content with whatever blessings or curses the computer and its priests cared to bestow on them.

With the centralized computer, users had access to only the software that the MIS (management information system) personnel chose to install. Often getting a new type of information out of that software required submitting a written request to the MIS priests and then waiting weeks for the results.

The personal computer—at least initially—seemed to be the beginning of the centralized computer's downfall. PC users could install on a PC whatever software they liked. The information users could extract from a PC was limited mostly by their skill with the software. And many users found that computing was really like the "great and powerful" Wizard of Oz: Once they got a peek behind the curtain that MIS had placed around computing, they found computers were just machines that weren't intimidating, after all.

More and more of the work that used to be done on mainframes and minicomputers wound up on PCs. Generally that has been all to the good, but the move away from centralized computing has a downside. When individuals work on stand-alone PCs, they work with stand-alone information. They lose the benefits of access to the information on the PC in the office next door. If a coworker does something that affects the data on which a business is based, the stand-alone PC user is left alone in the dark. Individual PCs do not reflect one very important aspect of the way most of us work—in cooperation with others.

The need to communicate and to share information with others gave rise to the PC network. With a network, you can retain the benefits of a personal computer—your own selections of software and a place for personal data not for sharing—and regain the benefits of centralized computing. With a network, you and your coworkers have the ability to work with the same latest version of the company's data and share selected information and messages.

Today the concept of a network is not limited to one location or even one business. The Internet, a network of networks, connects computer users around the world. You can run a program that resides on a PC on another continent and you can create your own "home page" that thousands of people you've never heard of can read.

Combining the benefits of PCs with those of networks is not a simple matter. The network becomes not only a link among personal computers—and often mainframes and minicomputers—but it must also act as a referee to arbitrate among conflicting requests for data and access to the network's resources.

Networking is new and arcane; it is filled with mysteries for most of those who use it. To explain all its workings, blessings, and failures would require its own book. Here we'll just examine some of the basics of network computing—how a network physically links individual PCs, the big picture of the Internet, and how networks use a special type of drive setup.

CHAPTER
27

How LAN Topologies Work

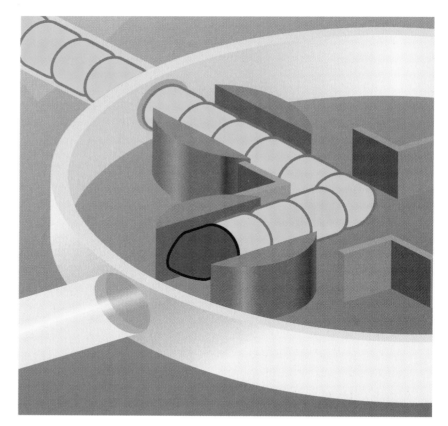

THE fundamental job of a LAN (local area network) is to physically link several PCs to each other and often to a mainframe or minicomputer. This is accomplished with a variety of materials—twisted-wire cables, fiber optics, phone lines, and even infrared light and radio signals.

There are nearly as many ways to link PCs logically as physically. Each network configuration—or *topology*—must still perform the same chores. The most common situation that a network encounters is a message from one PC to another. The message may be a query for data, the reply to another PC's data request, or an instruction to run a program that's stored on the network.

The data or program that the message asks for may be stored on a PC used by a coworker on the network, or on a file server, a specialized PC. A *file server* is usually a high-performance PC with a large hard drive that is not used exclusively by any individual on the network. Instead, it exists only to serve all the other PCs using the network—called clients—by providing a common place to store data that can be retrieved as rapidly as possible by the clients. Similarly, a network may include print servers that everyone on the LAN can use for printing. A *print server* is a PC connected to a printer or an intelligent printer that can be connected to a network without an intervening PC.

If a network does not have a dedicated server, it is a *peer-to-peer* network. In a peer-to-peer network, each individual's PC acts as a server to other PCs—its peers—on the network and is also a client to all its peers acting as servers.

The network must receive requests for access to it from individual PCs, or *nodes*, linked to the network, and the network must have a way of handling simultaneous requests for its services. Once a PC has the services of the network, the network needs a way of sending a message from one PC to another so that it goes only to the node it's intended for and doesn't pop up on some other unsuspecting PC. And the network must do all of this as quickly as possible while spreading its services as evenly as possible among all the nodes on the LAN.

Three network topologies—bus, token ring, and star—account for most LAN configurations, for both client-server and peer-to-peer networks. Here's how the different topologies handle service requests and conflicts.

Bus Network

1 All nodes on a bus, or Ethernet, network are attached to the LAN as branches off a common line. Each node has a unique address. The network card installed in a node, which can be another PC, a file server, or printer server, listens to make sure that no other signals are being transmitted along the network. It then sends a message to another device by giving it to a *transceiver*, usually on an expansion card. Each node has its own transceiver.

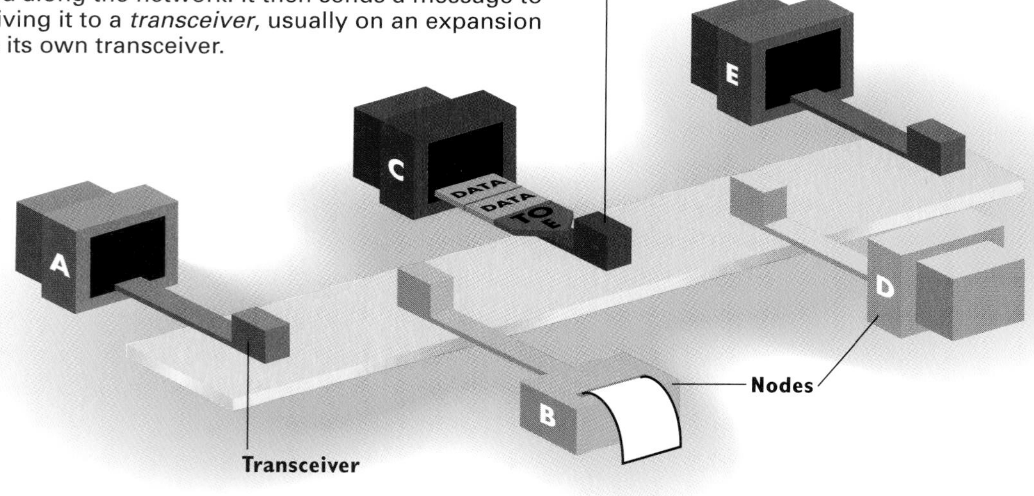

Nodes

Transceiver

2 The transceiver broadcasts the message in both directions so that it will reach all other nodes on the network. The message includes the addresses of its destination and source, error-checking packets, and the data itself.

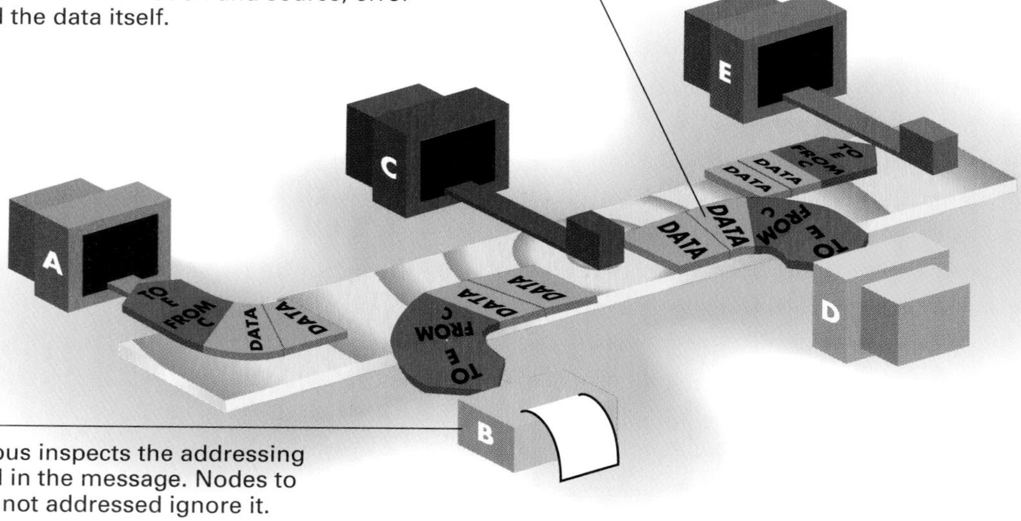

3 Each node along the bus inspects the addressing information contained in the message. Nodes to which the message is not addressed ignore it.

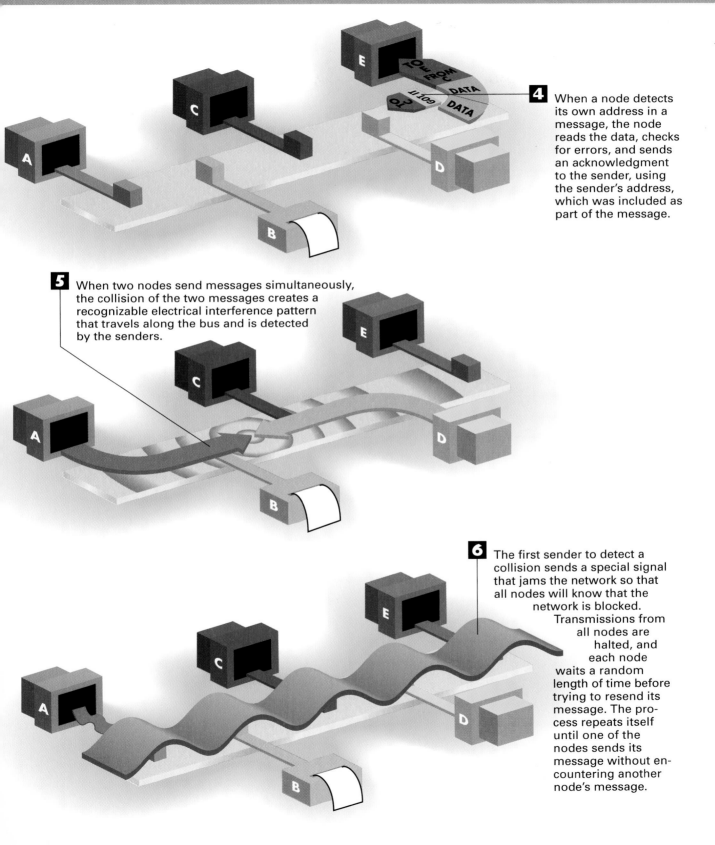

4 When a node detects its own address in a message, the node reads the data, checks for errors, and sends an acknowledgment to the sender, using the sender's address, which was included as part of the message.

5 When two nodes send messages simultaneously, the collision of the two messages creates a recognizable electrical interference pattern that travels along the bus and is detected by the senders.

6 The first sender to detect a collision sends a special signal that jams the network so that all nodes will know that the network is blocked. Transmissions from all nodes are halted, and each node waits a random length of time before trying to resend its message. The process repeats itself until one of the nodes sends its message without encountering another node's message.

Token-Ring Network

1 All nodes on a token-ring network are connected to the same circuit, which takes the form of a continuous loop. A token— which consists of a short all-clear message—circulates continuously around a loop and is read through a token-ring adapter card in each node as the token passes by.

2 A node wanting to send a message grabs the token as it passes by, changes the binary code in the token to say that it is in use, and attaches the node's message along with the address of the node for which the message is intended and the error-checking code. Only one message at a time can be circulated on the network.

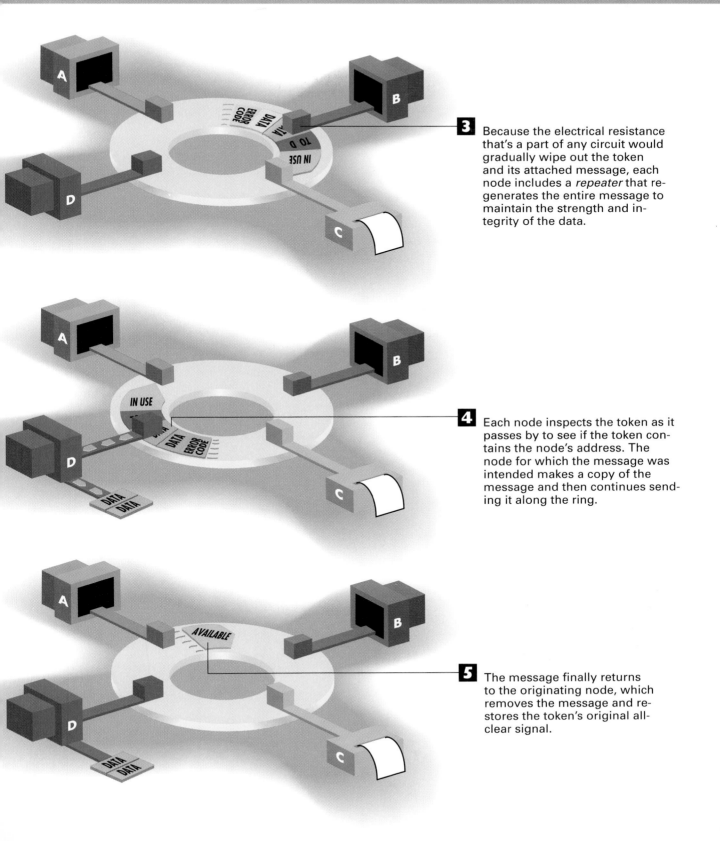

3 Because the electrical resistance that's a part of any circuit would gradually wipe out the token and its attached message, each node includes a *repeater* that regenerates the entire message to maintain the strength and integrity of the data.

4 Each node inspects the token as it passes by to see if the token contains the node's address. The node for which the message was intended makes a copy of the message and then continues sending it along the ring.

5 The message finally returns to the originating node, which removes the message and restores the token's original all-clear signal.

Star Network

1 Nodes in a star network configuration are attached to separate lines, all of which lead to the same hub or central station. The central station contains switches to connect any of the lines to any other line.

2 A node sends to the central station a message that includes the address of the node for which the message is intended and the data and error-checking code. More than one node can originate a message at the same time.

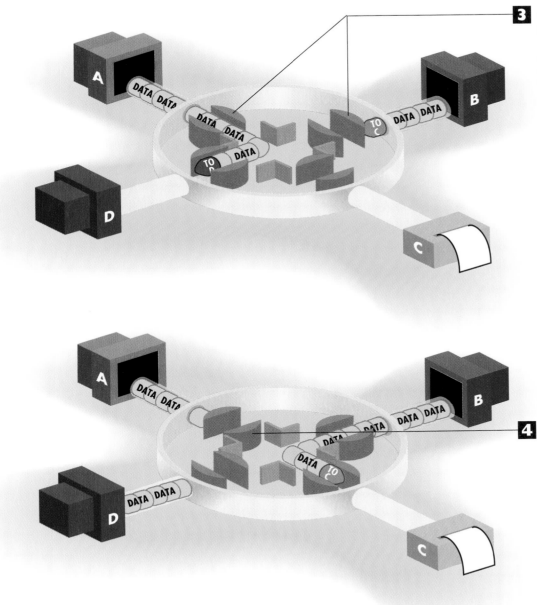

3 The switching station regularly polls each node connected to it. By taking turns opening and closing the switches, the station prevents any messages from colliding.

4 To prevent any one of the nodes from monopolizing the network, the switching station allows only a small portion of one message to pass through the switches at one time. Other messages are put on hold until the station comes around to them again.

CHAPTER 28

How the Internet Works

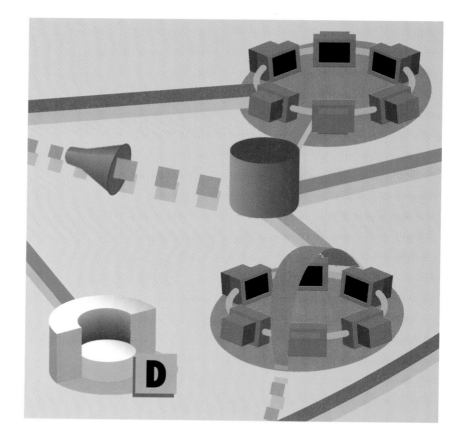

IT would be a lot easier to explain how the Internet, or the Net, works if you could hold it in your hand. Hardware—real, tangible, with a weight and size—is always easier to understand because you can see it and you can point with confidence to say this gizmo leads to that gadget, every time. The Internet is not just a single thing. It is an *abstract system*. To understand the significance of this term, consider a less abstract system—your body.

The molecules that make up your body are not the same all your life. New molecules are constantly being taken in as food, water, and air and recombined into different molecules of muscle, blood, and bone. But no matter which molecules make up your hair and eyes and fingers at any moment, the *structure* of your body remains the same. Your heart doesn't refuse to pump because new molecules of blood are created. If you remove some parts of your body, the system continues to function, sometimes, as in the case of brain damage, transferring the job of the missing parts to healthy parts of the brain.

As a system, the Internet is similar to a living organism. It grows, taking in new "molecules" in the form of PCs and networks that attach themselves to the Net. Parts of the Internet communicate with other parts that then respond with some action, not unlike the muscle activity set off by nerve impulses. You can think of the Internet as a network of networks. Amoeba-like, smaller networks can break off the Net and live independent lives. Unlike amoebas, those smaller networks can rejoin the main body of the Net.

The Net is ephemeral. Some pieces—the supercomputers that form the backbone of the Internet—are always there. But nothing is really hard-wired, fixed. Each time you use your PC to connect with, say, a PC in Pittsburgh that maintains information on "Star Trek," you don't have to use the same phone lines, switching devices, and intermediate networks to reach it. Without realizing it, you may, in fact, be bounced back and forth among several networks from one end of the county to the other until you reach your destination in cyberspace.

It's a lot easier to say what you can get from the Net: conceivably anything. Being a system without physical limitations, it's theoretically possible for the Net to include all information on all computers everywhere, which in this age means essentially everything the human race knows, or thinks it knows. But because the Net is such an ad-hoc system, exploring it can be a challenge. And you don't always find exactly what you want. There are plenty of software tools that make surfing the Net easier, but the Internet itself has no overall design to help those using it. You're pretty much on your own when you jump in with whatever software you can find.

Despite the amorphous nature of the individual elements that make up the Internet, it is possible to describe the structure of the Net—the system that always remains the same while the elements that make it up change.

How the Internet Makes Connections

5 As the request passes from network to network, a set of *protocols*, or rules, create *packets*. Packets contain the data itself as well as the addresses, error checking, and other information needed to make sure the request arrives intact at the proper destination.

4 Several networks in the same region may be grouped into a *mid-level* network. If your request is destined for another system within the same mid-level network, the router sends it on directly to its destination. This is sometimes done through high-speed phone lines, fiber-optic connections, and microwave links. A variation, called a *wide area network* (WAN), covers a larger geographical area and may incorporate connections through orbiting satellites

3 A router is a device on a network that connects networks and inspects your request to determine what other part of the Internet it's addressed to. Then, based on available connections and the traffic on different parts of the Net, the router determines the best path to the request's destination.

2 Your *host* network makes a connection on another line to a separate network nearby. Or, if the second network is some distance away, your host LAN may go through a *router*.

1 Your PC makes a connection to a *local area network* (LAN). This happens either by being directly wired to the network or by using a modem to connect via a telephone to another modem that is wired directly to the network. Either way, you request data contained somewhere else on the Internet.

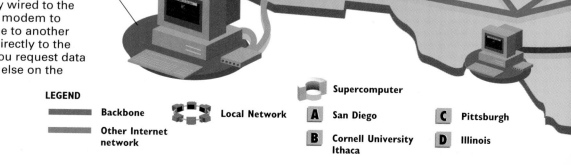

LEGEND

▬▬ Backbone	Local Network	Supercomputer
▬▬ Other Internet network	**A** San Diego	**C** Pittsburgh
	B Cornell University Ithaca	**D** Illinois

6 If the destination for your request isn't on the same mid-level network or WAN as your host network, the router sends the request to a network access point (NAP). The pathway may take any of several routes along the Internet's *backbone*, a collection of networks that link extremely powerful supercomputers associated with the National Science Foundation. The Internet, however, isn't limited to the United States. You can connect to computers on the Net in virtually any part of the world. Along the way, your request may pass through repeaters, hubs, bridges, and gateways.

Repeaters amplify or refresh the stream of data, which deteriorates the farther it travels from your PC. Repeaters let the data signals reach more remote PCs.

Hubs link groups of networks so that the personal computers and terminals attached to each of those networks can talk to any of the other networks.

Bridges link LANs so that data from one network can pass through another network on its way to still a third LAN.

Gateways are similar to bridges. They also translate data between one type of network and another, such as Netware running on a DOS-based system, and Banyan Vines running on a Unix system.

7 When the request reaches its destination, the packets of data, addresses, and error-correction are read. The remote computer then takes the appropriate action, such as running a program, sending data back to your PC, or posting a message on the Internet.

Other important stops on the Internet

E SUNY at Buffalo

F OCEANIC: University of Delaware

G Minnesota Computer Center

H University of British Columbia

I University of Washington Information Navigator

J PORTALS: Portland Area Library Services

K Stanford Linear Accelerator

L NASA Ames Research Center

M Weather Underground, University of Colorado

CHAPTER

29

How a Drive Array Works

DRIVE arrays work on the theory that if one hard drive is a good thing, two hard drives are twice as good, and five hard drives are five times as good. By using multiple hard drives configured so the operating system thinks they are only a single drive, a network server can achieve greater speed reading data from the drives or greater protection from data loss. Ideally, you can achieve both economically.

The most common type of drive array is a *RAID*, an acronym for *redundant array of inexpensive drives*. The cost of hard drives increases with capacity and speed. But with a RAID, you can use several cheaper drives whose total cost is less than one high-performance drive and attain similar performance with greater data security.

RAIDs use some combination of mirroring and/or striping; both methods provide greater protection from lost data. *Mirroring*, in which one drive is a direct copy of another drive, provides the greatest performance enhancement but at the greatest cost. *Striping*, in which files are spread over several drives and protected with data on still another drive, is used when data protection is needed in addition to a good performance boost.

Traditionally, drive arrays have been used only rarely on stand-alone PCs because, despite the tactic of using low-cost drivers, the array as a whole is still expensive compared to the cost of most individual PC components. Arrays are almost always found on PCs used as network servers.

Mirrored Drive Array

1 When a file is written to a mirrored drive array, the controller simultaneously sends identical copies of the file to each drive in the array. A mirrored array can consist of as few as two drives.

2 When a file is to be read from a mirrored array, the controller reads alternate file clusters simultaneously from each of the drives and pieces them together for delivery to the PC. This process makes reads faster. How fast depends on the number of drives in the array. If two drives are mirrored, read time is cut approximately in half; three mirrored drives reduce read time to about one-third that of a single drive.

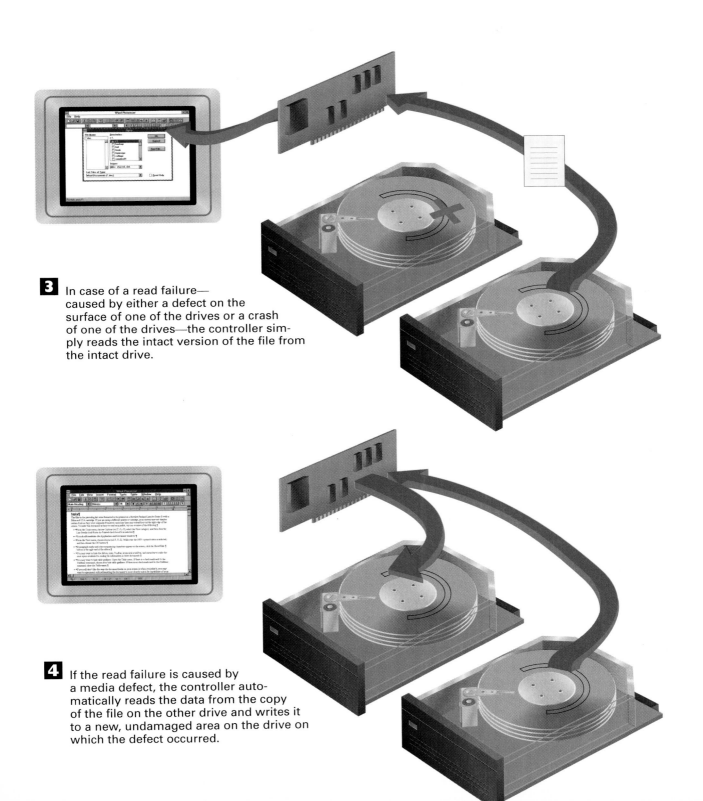

3 In case of a read failure—caused by either a defect on the surface of one of the drives or a crash of one of the drives—the controller simply reads the intact version of the file from the intact drive.

4 If the read failure is caused by a media defect, the controller automatically reads the data from the copy of the file on the other drive and writes it to a new, undamaged area on the drive on which the defect occurred.

Striped Drive Array

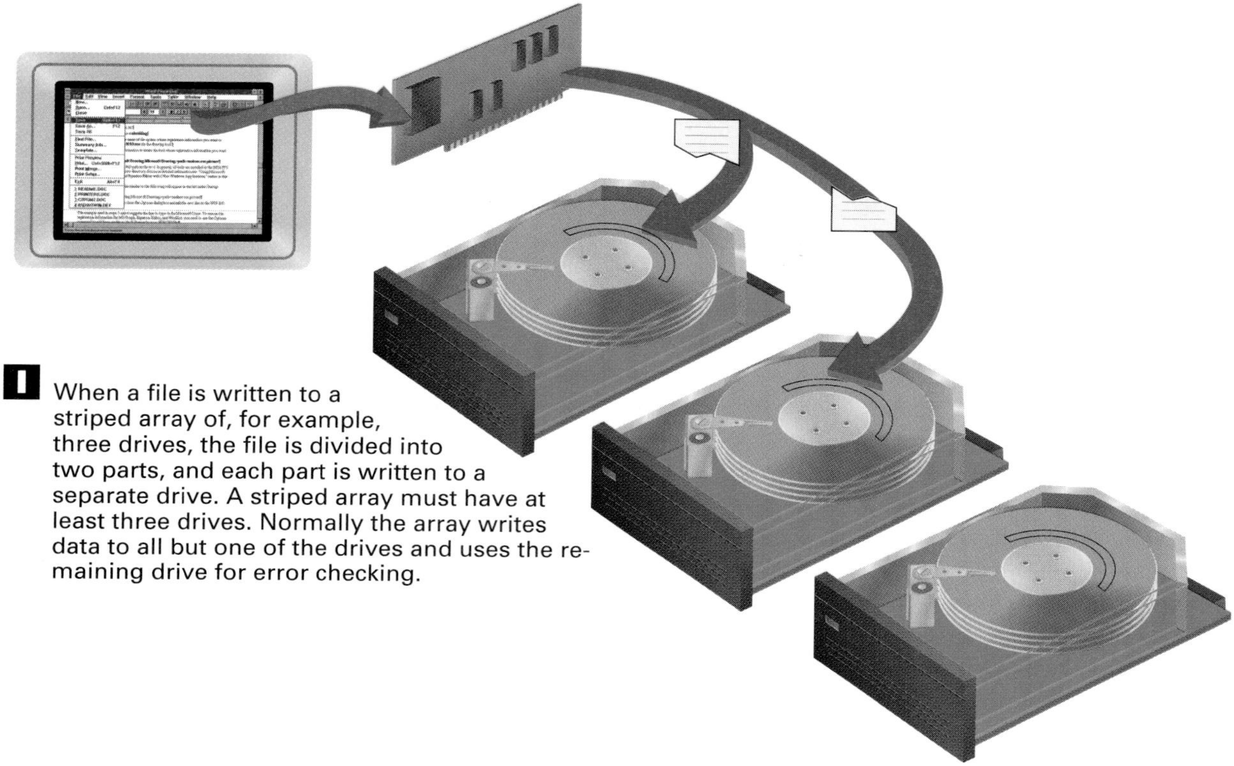

1 When a file is written to a striped array of, for example, three drives, the file is divided into two parts, and each part is written to a separate drive. A striped array must have at least three drives. Normally the array writes data to all but one of the drives and uses the remaining drive for error checking.

2 The controller or array software performs a Boolean XOR operation on the data written to the drives and writes the result, often called a parity bit, to the remaining drive. An XOR operation results in a 0 bit whenever two like bits are compared and a 1 bit whenever two dissimilar bits are compared. For example, XORing the two binary numbers 1100 and 1010 yields the parity 0110. If more than three drives are in an array, first two are XORed and then that result is XORed with the next drive, and so on until all the drives containing data have been XORed and the final result written to the parity drive. This operation negates much of the performance improvement achieved in the first step by simultaneously writing different parts of the file.

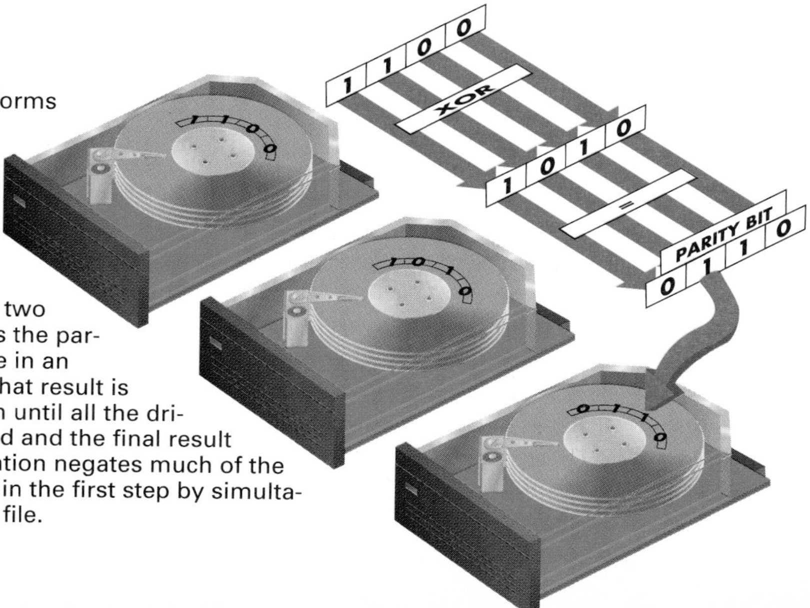

1 1 0 0
XOR
1 0 1 0
=
PARITY BIT
0 1 1 0

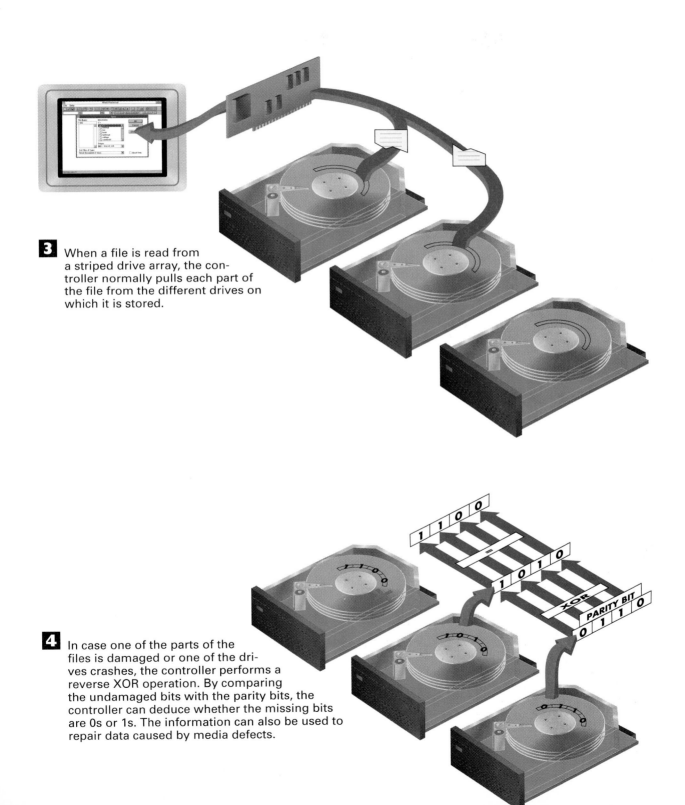

3 When a file is read from a striped drive array, the controller normally pulls each part of the file from the different drives on which it is stored.

4 In case one of the parts of the files is damaged or one of the drives crashes, the controller performs a reverse XOR operation. By comparing the undamaged bits with the parity bits, the controller can deduce whether the missing bits are 0s or 1s. The information can also be used to repair data caused by media defects.

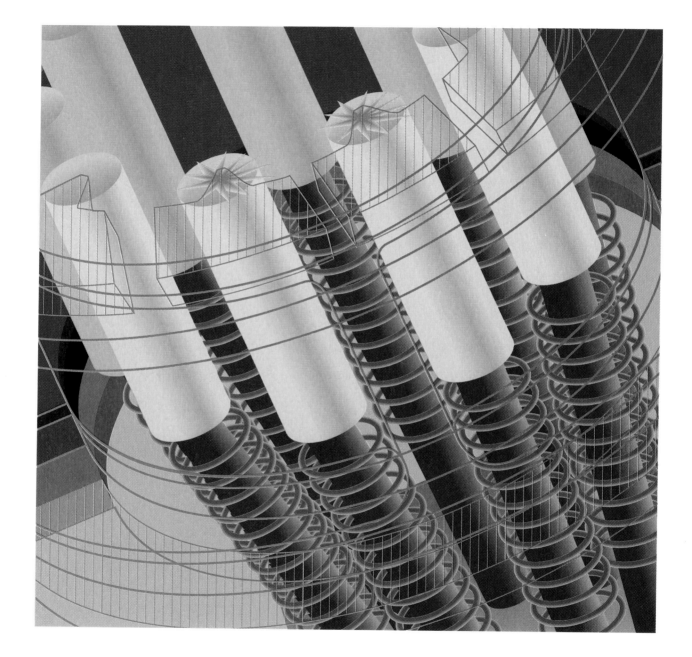

P A R T

PRINTERS

IN the early days of personal computers, someone came up with the idea that all this computerized data would lead to the "paperless office." We're more than a decade into the personal computer revolution and more trees than ever are giving their lives to produce hard copies of everything from company budgets complete with full-color graphs to homemade greeting cards. Not only are we creating more printouts than ever before, but computer printing has turned into a fine art. The very essence of a whole new category of software—desktop publishing—is the accomplishment of better and better printed pages.

Whoever made that erroneous prediction about a paperless office missed an important fact. That person was probably thinking about how offices used paper in the age of the typewriter. Then there wasn't much you could put on paper except black letters and numbers—most often in an efficient but drab typeface called Courier. If all those ugly memos and letters had been replaced by electronic mail, the world would not have suffered a great loss. But what happened is that most people didn't predict back then that software and printing technology would make possible the fast, easy hard-copy versions of reports, newsletters, graphs, and, yes, memos and letters that even IBM's best Selectric could never come close to producing.

Speed and ease were the first improvements in printing. Where a simple typo on a typewriter might just be whited out or hand-corrected with a pen, today—because of the speed of printers—it's easier just to correct a mistake on screen and print a fresh, flawless copy.

Graphics were the next big advance. The day of the all-text document ended with the first software that could print even the crudest line graph on a dot-matrix printer. Now anything that's visual, from line art to halftone photograph, can be printed on a standard office printer.

Today, color is the current frontier being conquered with office printers. The quality and speed of color printers is increasing as their cost is decreasing. Because black-and-white printers are getting even faster and cheaper, we aren't likely to see color printers entirely replace monochrome printers, but they will start showing up in more offices on networks where they can be shared.

And, paper hasn't disappeared from the office. Instead, it's taken on a whole new importance. And the lowly printer that used to turn out crude approximations of characters is now one of the most important components of a computer system.

CHAPTER 30

How Bitmapped and Outline Fonts Work

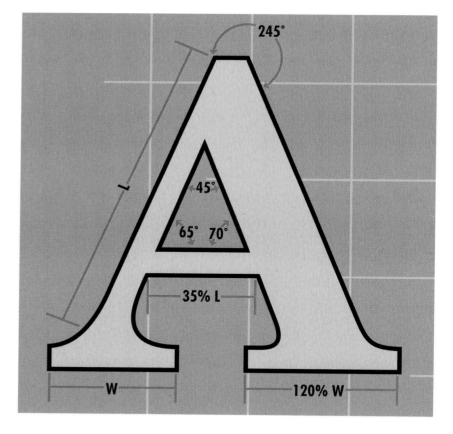

ALL printers, whether dot-matrix, ink-jet, laser, or thermal, accomplish essentially the same task: They create a pattern of dots on a sheet of paper. The dots may be sized differently or composed of different inks transferred to the paper by different means, but all of the images for text and graphics are made up of dots. The smaller the dots, the more attractive the end result will be.

Regardless of how the dots are created on paper, there has to be a common scheme for determining where to place the dots; the most common schemes are bitmaps and outline fonts. Bitmapped fonts come in predefined sizes and weights. Outline fonts can be scaled and given special attributes, such as boldfacing and underlining, on the fly. Each has its advantages and disadvantages, depending on what type of output you want.

Bitmapped images are generally limited to text and are a fast way to produce a printed page that uses only a few type fonts. If the hard copy is to include a graphic image in addition to bitmapped text, then, to create the graphic, your software must be able to send the printer instructions that it will understand.

Outline fonts are used with a page description language that treats everything on a page—even text—as a graphic. The text and graphics used by the software are converted to a series of commands that the printer's page description language uses to determine where each dot is to be placed on a page. Page description languages generally are slower at producing hard copy, but they are more versatile at producing different sizes of type with different attributes or special effects, and they create more attractive results.

Bitmapped Fonts

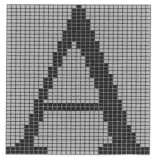

36 pt. medium

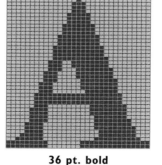

36 pt. bold

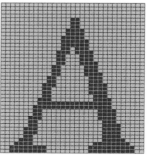

30 pt. medium

1 Bit-mapped fonts are typefaces of a certain size and with specific attributes or characteristics, such as boldface or italic. The bitmap is a record of the pattern of dots needed to create a specific character in a certain size and with a certain attribute. The bitmaps for a 36-point Times Roman medium capital *A*, for a 36-point Times Roman boldface capital *A*, and for a 30-point Times Roman medium capital *A* are all different and specific.

Cartridge

2 Most printers come with a few bitmapped fonts—usually Courier and Line Printer—in both normal and boldface varieties as part of their permanent memory (ROM). In addition, many printers have random access memory (RAM) to which your computer can send bitmaps for other fonts. You can also add additional bitmapped fonts in the form of plug-in cartridges used by many laser printers.

3 When you issue a print command—either from your operating system or from within your application software—to a printer using bitmapped fonts, your PC first tells the printer which of the bitmap tables contained in memory to use.

4 Then for each letter, punctuation mark, or paper movement—such as a tab or carriage return—that the software wants the printer to create, the PC sends an ASCII code. ASCII codes consist of hexadecimal numbers that are matched against the table of bitmaps. (Hexadecimal numbers have a base of 16—1, 2, 3, 4, 5, 6, 7, 8, 9, 0, A, B, C, D, E, F—instead of the base 10 used by decimal numbers.) If, for example, the hexadecimal number 41 (65 decimal) is sent to the printer, the printer's processor looks up 41h in its table and finds that it corresponds to a pattern of dots that creates an uppercase *A* in whatever typeface, type size, and attribute is in the active table.

BITMAP TABLE	
39h	
40h	
41h	A
42h	B
43h	C

41h

5 The printer uses that bitmap to determine which instructions to send to its other components to reproduce the bitmap's pattern on paper. Each character, one after the other, is sent to the printer.

Outline Fonts

36pt

245°

45°

65° 70°

35% L

W — 120% W

24pt

245°

45°

65° 70°

35% L

W — 120% W

1 Outline fonts, unlike bitmapped fonts, are not limited to specific sizes and attributes of a typeface. Instead, they consist of mathematical descriptions of each character and punctuation mark in a typeface. They are called outline fonts because the outline of a Times Roman 36-point capital *A* is proportionally the same as that of a 24-point Times Roman capital *A*.

```
/_ieq    {gsave
   dup /picstr exch 7 add idiv string def
   3 1 roll translate dup 1 scale
   dup 1 false [5 -1 roll 0 0 1 0 0]
   {currentfile picstr readhexstring pop}
   grestore} bdef
letter _bp 0 13200 10200
0 13200 10200 _ornt
/_r      { stlg }/_t {0 rmoveto}bdef
         {/_s /show load def /_t {0
def}ifelse
   }bdef
1200 11863 _m
/Courier-BoldR 600 _ff

{Now}_S 120 _t
{is}_S 120 _t
{the}_S 120 _t
{time}_S 120 _t
{for}_S120 _t
   /Courier-BoldObliqueR 600 _ff
```

2 Some printers come with a page description language, most commonly PostScript or Hewlett-Packard Printer Command Language, in *firmware*—a computer program contained on a microchip. The language can translate outline font commands from your PC's software into the instructions the printer needs to control where it places dots on a sheet of paper. For printers that don't have a built-in page description language, PC software can translate the printer language commands into the instructions the printer needs.

$$\frac{(X-Y)+.75X}{\cos(A)}$$

3 When you issue a print command from your application software to a printer using outline fonts, your application sends a series of commands the page description language interprets through a set of algorithms, or mathematical formulas. The algorithms describe the lines and arcs that make up the characters in a typeface. The algorithms for some typefaces include *hints*, special alterations to the outlines if the type is to be either extremely big or extremely small.

4 The commands insert variables into the formulas to change the size or attributes of the outline font. The results are commands to the printer that say, in effect, "Create a horizontal line 3 points wide, which begins 60 points from the bottom and 20 points to the right." The page description language turns on all the bits that fall inside the outline of the letter—unless the font includes some special shading effect within the outline.

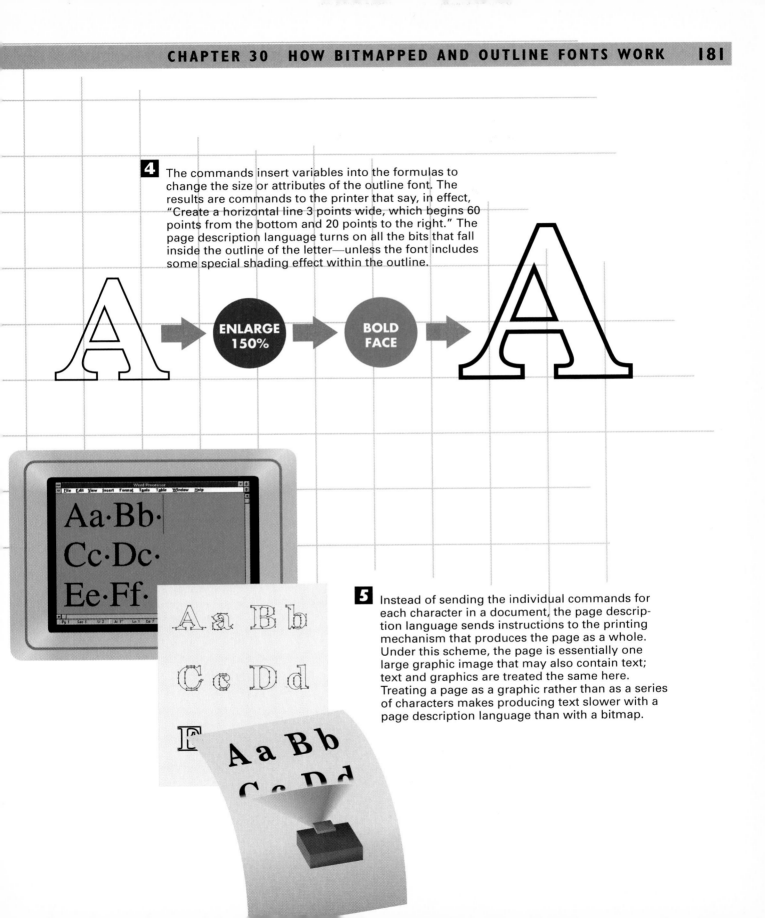

ENLARGE 150%

BOLD FACE

5 Instead of sending the individual commands for each character in a document, the page description language sends instructions to the printing mechanism that produces the page as a whole. Under this scheme, the page is essentially one large graphic image that may also contain text; text and graphics are treated the same here. Treating a page as a graphic rather than as a series of characters makes producing text slower with a page description language than with a bitmap.

CHAPTER
31

How a Dot-Matrix Printer Works

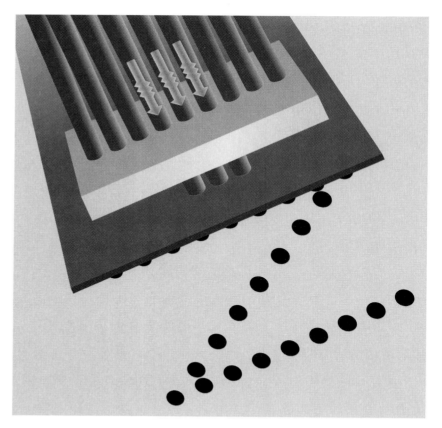

ALTHOUGH

laser printers are faster and produce more attractive documents, the mechanical dot-matrix printer continues to be a mainstay of many computer systems. Laser printers often cost $600–$1,000; a reliable dot-matrix printer costs only a few hundred. Laser printers require replacing a toner cartridge that costs nearly as much as a low-end dot-matrix printer; all a dot-matrix printer needs in the way of supplies is a new ribbon, now and then, which you can buy for pocket change.

Dot-matrix printers are a necessity for tasks that require printing on multilayer forms, something the nonimpact laser printer can't do at all. And today's 24-pin dot-matrix printers increase both the printer's speed and the quality of the type.

Manufacturers continue to introduce newer, faster, more intelligent—even less noisy—dot-matrix printers to receptive users. Chances are good that dot-matrix impact printers will stay with us for years to come.

Although some dot-matrix printers can interpret commands from PostScript or some other page description language, most impact printers are designed to work with bitmapped type controlled by ASCII codes sent to the printer from a PC. (See "How Bitmapped and Outline Fonts Work" for details on page description languages and bitmapped type.)

Dot-Matrix Printer

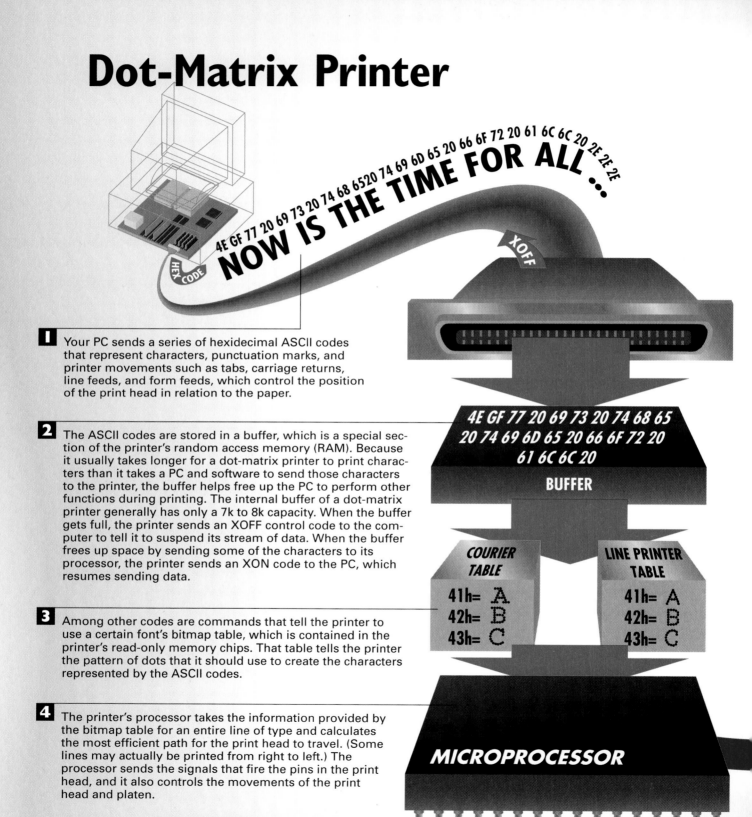

4E GF 77 20 69 73 20 74 68 6520 74 69 6D 65 20 66 6F 72 20 61 6C 6C 20 2E 2E 2E

NOW IS THE TIME FOR ALL ...

HEX CODE

XOFF

1 Your PC sends a series of hexidecimal ASCII codes that represent characters, punctuation marks, and printer movements such as tabs, carriage returns, line feeds, and form feeds, which control the position of the print head in relation to the paper.

2 The ASCII codes are stored in a buffer, which is a special section of the printer's random access memory (RAM). Because it usually takes longer for a dot-matrix printer to print characters than it takes a PC and software to send those characters to the printer, the buffer helps free up the PC to perform other functions during printing. The internal buffer of a dot-matrix printer generally has only a 7k to 8k capacity. When the buffer gets full, the printer sends an XOFF control code to the computer to tell it to suspend its stream of data. When the buffer frees up space by sending some of the characters to its processor, the printer sends an XON code to the PC, which resumes sending data.

3 Among other codes are commands that tell the printer to use a certain font's bitmap table, which is contained in the printer's read-only memory chips. That table tells the printer the pattern of dots that it should use to create the characters represented by the ASCII codes.

4 The printer's processor takes the information provided by the bitmap table for an entire line of type and calculates the most efficient path for the print head to travel. (Some lines may actually be printed from right to left.) The processor sends the signals that fire the pins in the print head, and it also controls the movements of the print head and platen.

4E GF 77 20 69 73 20 74 68 65
20 74 69 6D 65 20 66 6F 72 20
61 6C 6C 20

BUFFER

COURIER TABLE

41h= A
42h= B
43h= C

LINE PRINTER TABLE

41h= A
42h= B
43h= C

MICROPROCESSOR

5 Electrical signals from the processor are amplified and travel to certain of the circuits that lead to the print head. The print head contains 9 or 24 wires, called printing pins, that are aligned in one or two straight lines. One end of each of the pins is matched to an individual *solenoid*, or electromagnet. The current from the processor activates the solenoid, which creates a magnetic field that repels a magnet on the end of the pin, causing the pin to move toward the paper.

6 The moving pin strikes a ribbon that is coated with ink. The force of the impact transfers ink to the paper on the other side of the ribbon. After the pin fires, a spring pulls it back to its original position. The print head continues firing different combinations of print wires as it moves across the page so that all characters are made up of various vertical dot patterns. Some printers improve print quality or create boldface by moving the print head through a second pass over the same line of type to print a second set of dots that are offset slightly from the first set.

C H A P T E R
32

How a Laser Printer Works

EVERY time you send a page to your laser printer, you're setting in motion a complex series of steps as efficiently organized as a factory and as precisely choreographed as a ballet.

At the heart of the printer is the *print engine*—the mechanism that transfers a black powder to the page—which is a device that owes its ancestry to the photocopier. Its parts represent the highest state of printing technology, including laser imaging, precise paper movement, and microprocessor control of all its actions.

To create the nearly typeset-quality output that is characteristic of a laser printer, the printer must control five different operations at the same time: (1) It must interpret the signals coming from a computer, (2) translate those signals into instructions that control the firing and movement of a laser beam, (3) control the movement of the paper, (4) sensitize the paper so that it will accept the black toner that makes up the image, and (5) fuse that image to the paper.

The result is no-compromise printing. Not only does the laser printer produce hard copy faster than does the dot-matrix printer, but the laser-printed pages are more sharply detailed than those of most dot-matrixes. The laser printer, for the foreseeable future, represents the standard for high-end computerized printing.

Laser Printer

2 The instructions from the printer's processor rapidly turn on and off a beam of light from a laser.

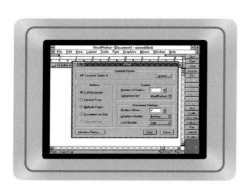

1 Your PC's operating system or software sends signals to the laser printer to determine where each dot of printing toner is to be placed on the paper. The signals are one of two types—either a simple ASCII code or a page description language command. (See Chapter 30, "How Bitmapped and Outline Fonts Work.")

10 The paper train pushes the paper out of the printer, usually with the printed side down so that pages end up in the output tray in the correct order.

9 Another set of rollers pulls the paper through a part of the print engine called the *fusing system*. There pressure and heat bind the toner permanently to the paper by melting and pressing a wax that is part of the toner. The heat from the fusing system is what causes paper fresh from a laser printer to be warm.

8 The rotation of the drum brings its surface next to a thin wire called the *corona wire*. It's called that because electricity passing through the wire creates a ring, or corona, around it that has a positive charge. The corona returns the entire surface of the drum to its original negative charge so that another page can be drawn on the drum's surface by the laser beam.

3 A spinning mirror deflects the laser beam so that the path of the beam is a horizontal line across the surface of a cylinder called the *organic photoconducting cartridge* (*OPC*), usually referred to as simply the *drum*. The combination of the laser beam being turned on and off and the movement of the beam's path across the cylinder results in many tiny points of light hitting in a line across the surface of the drum. When the laser has finished flashing points of light across the entire width of the OPC, the drum rotates—usually 1/300th–1/600th of an inch in most laser printers—and the laser beam begins working on the next line of dots.

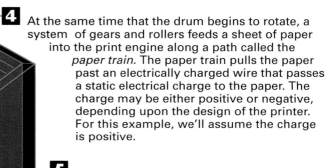

4 At the same time that the drum begins to rotate, a system of gears and rollers feeds a sheet of paper into the print engine along a path called the *paper train*. The paper train pulls the paper past an electrically charged wire that passes a static electrical charge to the paper. The charge may be either positive or negative, depending upon the design of the printer. For this example, we'll assume the charge is positive.

5 Where each point of light strikes the drum, it causes a negatively charged film—usually made of zinc oxide and other materials—on the surface of the drum to change its charge so that the dots have the same electrical charge as the sheet of paper. In this example, the light would change the charge from negative to positive. Each positive charge marks a dot that eventually will print black on paper (see Note below for information about write-white printers). The areas of the drum that remain untouched by the laser beam retain their negative charge and result in white areas on the hard copy.

6 About halfway through the drum's rotation, the OPC comes into contact with a bin that contains a black powder called *toner*. The toner in this example has a negative electrical charge—the opposite of the charges created on the drum by the laser beam. Because particles with opposite static charges attract each other, toner sticks to the drum in a pattern of small dots wherever the laser beam created a charge.

7 As the drum continues to turn, it presses against the sheet of paper being fed along the paper train. Although the electrical charge on the paper is the same as the charge of the drum created by the laser beam, the paper's charge is stronger and pulls the toner off the drum and onto the paper.

NOTE In the description above, the electrical charges in all instances can be reversed and the result would be much the same. The method described here is true of most printers that use the Canon print engine, such as Hewlett-Packard models, which are the standard among laser printers. This approach is called *write-black* because every dot etched on the printer drum by the laser beam marks a place that will be black on the printout. However, there is an alternative way that a laser printer can work and that way produces noticeably different results. The other method, used by Ricoh print engines, is called *write-white* because everywhere the laser beam strikes, it creates a charge the same as that of the toner—the toner is attracted to the areas not affected by the beam of light. Write-white printers generally produce darker black areas, and write-black printers generally produce finer details.

CHAPTER

33

How a Color Ink-Jet Printer Works

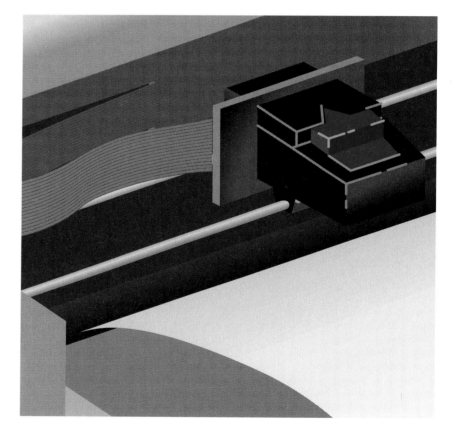

INK-JET printers occupy a niche between dot-matrix impact printers and laser printers. These small printers that fit on nearly any desk share the fine resolution of laser printers. Only with the closest inspection are you likely to detect the difference between laser and ink-jet output.

And like laser devices, ink-jets spare you the insect whine and chatter that accompany impact printers. All you hear is a slight whisper followed by a low thunk as a page is ejected.

For all the similarity between the output of ink-jet and laser printers, ink-jets really more resemble dot-matrix printers. They both have print heads that travel across the width of a page, depositing an entire line of text with each pass. (See "How a Dot-Matrix Printer Works" for more details on how printing commands are interpreted by any printer that uses a matrix print head.) This mechanical movement puts ink-jet printers in the same speed class as impact printers, but ink-jets deposit ink in much smaller dots than do impact printers. The price of ink-jets is usually close to that of dot-matrix printers. They are the perfect compromise of cost, speed, and quality.

The biggest difference between ink-jet printers and both of its cousins is the ink-jet's print head. Using a technology so unusual that you wonder how anyone ever thought of it, an ink-jet printer spits little drops of ink onto paper. It's a technology that works much better than you would imagine and also lends itself readily to inexpensive color printing.

Color Ink-Jet Printer

1 An ink-filled print cartridge attached to the ink-jet's print head moves sideways across the width of a sheet of paper that is fed through the printer below the print head.

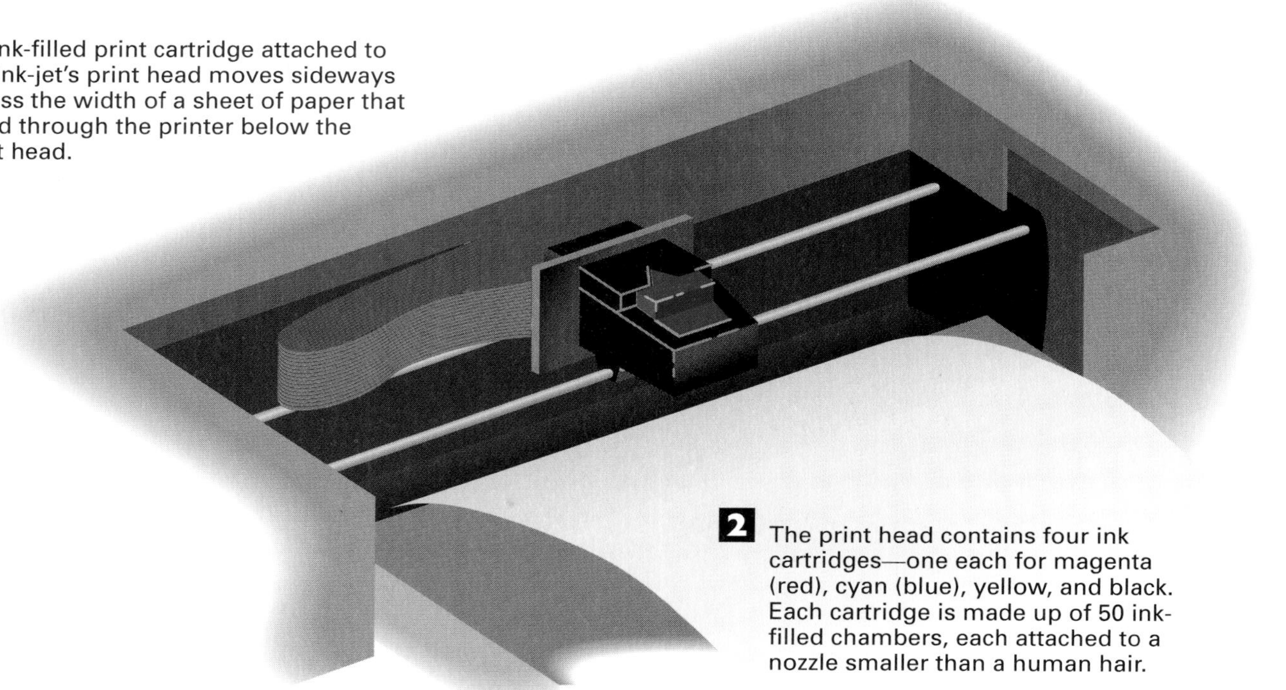

2 The print head contains four ink cartridges—one each for magenta (red), cyan (blue), yellow, and black. Each cartridge is made up of 50 ink-filled chambers, each attached to a nozzle smaller than a human hair.

3 An electrical pulse flows through thin resistors at the bottom of all the chambers that the printer will use to form a character on paper.

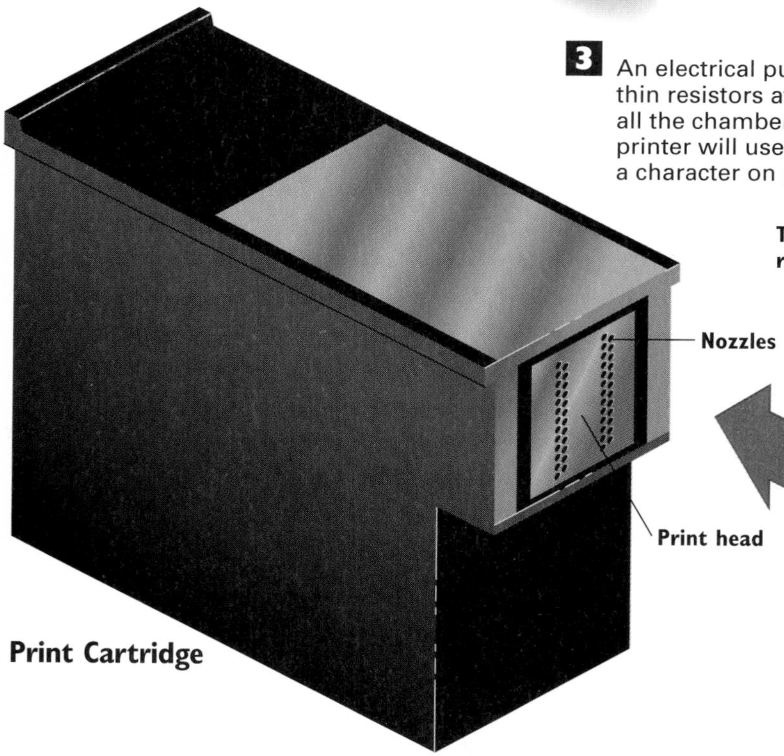

Thin film resistor

Nozzles

Print head

Ink from reservoir

Firing chamber   Nozzle

Print Cartridge

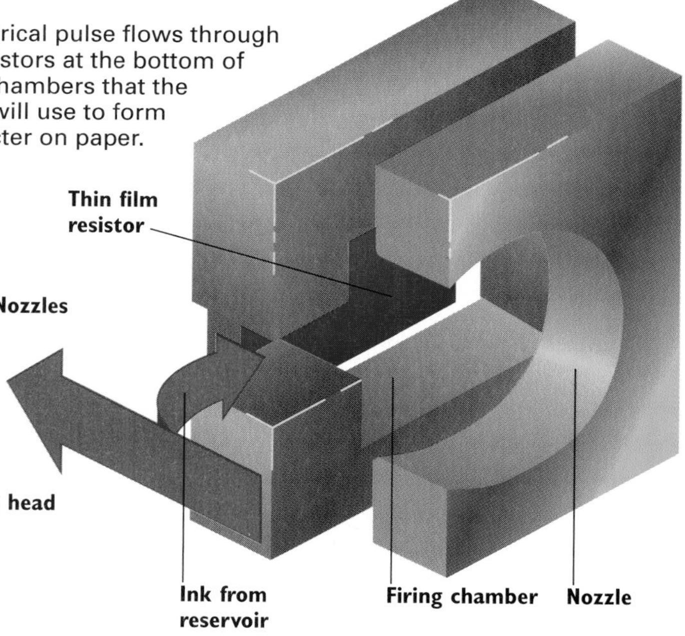

Nozzle Cross Section

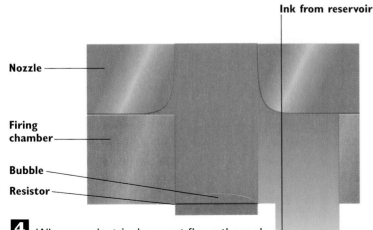

Ink from reservoir

Nozzle

Firing chamber

Bubble

Resistor

4 When an electrical current flows through a resistor, the resistor heats a thin layer of ink at the bottom of the chamber to more than 900 degrees Fahrenheit for several millionths of a second. The ink boils and forms a bubble of vapor.

5 As the vapor bubble expands, it pushes ink through the nozzle to form a droplet at the tip of the nozzle.

Paper

Droplet

Ink dot

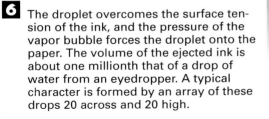

6 The droplet overcomes the surface tension of the ink, and the pressure of the vapor bubble forces the droplet onto the paper. The volume of the ejected ink is about one millionth that of a drop of water from an eyedropper. A typical character is formed by an array of these drops 20 across and 20 high.

7 As the resistor cools, the bubble collapses. The resulting suction pulls fresh ink from the attached reservoir into the firing chamber.

CHAPTER

34

How a Wax Thermal Printer Works

FAST,

FAST, inexpensive color printing is the holy grail of printer manufacturers. Although color printers are getting faster, smaller, and less expensive, the very nature of combining colors on the same sheet of paper automatically makes the process complicated.

Anytime you look at a color-printed page, you're actually looking at a complex arrangement of only four colors of ink—cyan (blue), magenta (red), yellow, and black. (Sometimes black is not included because a printer can create black—usually with not entirely satisfactory results—by combining equal portions of the other three colors.) If you look closely at a magnified section of a color-printed page, you'll see a pattern of colored dots.

Because each printed color is made up of at least three separate colors, each page must, in effect, be printed at least three times. To the time it takes to perform all these mechanical movements, add the processing time your software requires to figure out the correct mixtures of colors and generate the instructions to the printer, and the result is an invariably slow process.

Some of the earliest color printers were based on variations of the techniques used in traditional black printing. Dot-matrix impact printers use ribbons with three or four bands of colored ink. Ink-jet printers use three or four print heads, each with an accompanying cartridge of colored ink. The most recent development has been color laser printers, which run paper past separate toners for each color.

The most common professional color-printing device in use is the color thermal printer, shown here. The process provides vivid colors because the inks it uses don't bleed into each other or soak into specially coated paper.

Color Thermal Printer

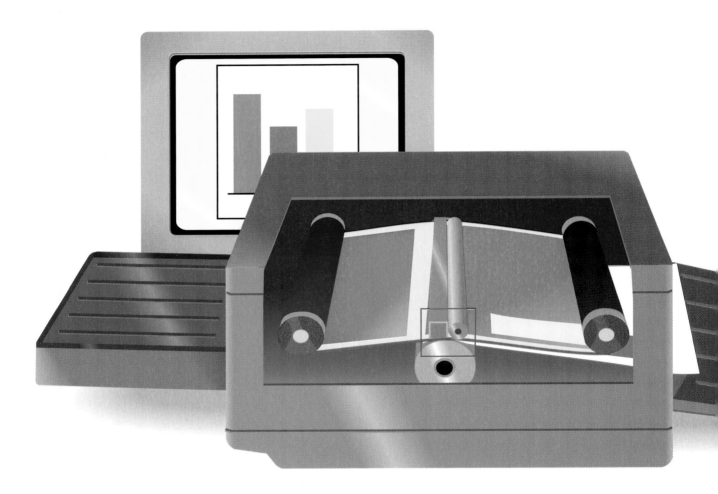

1 The color thermal printer feeds a sheet of specially coated paper from its bin into the print engine, where the paper is held on one side by a roller that presses the paper against a wide ribbon coated with colored inks mixed with wax or plastic. The ribbon contains a band of each of the composite printing colors—cyan, magenta, yellow and, if it's used, black. Each color band covers a large area—the width and length of the sheet of paper.

2 As the paper passes through the paper train, it first presses against the cyan band of the ribbon. One or more heating elements arranged in a row on the thermal print head on the other side of the ribbon are turned on and melt small dots of the cyan dye. The melted dots are pressed against the paper.

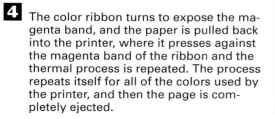

3 The paper continues moving through the paper train until it is partially ejected from the printer. As the paper peels away from the ribbon, the unmelted cyan ink remains on the ribbon and the melted dye sticks to the paper.

4 The color ribbon turns to expose the magenta band, and the paper is pulled back into the printer, where it presses against the magenta band of the ribbon and the thermal process is repeated. The process repeats itself for all of the colors used by the printer, and then the page is completely ejected.

CHAPTER
35

How a Dye-Sublimation Color Printer Works

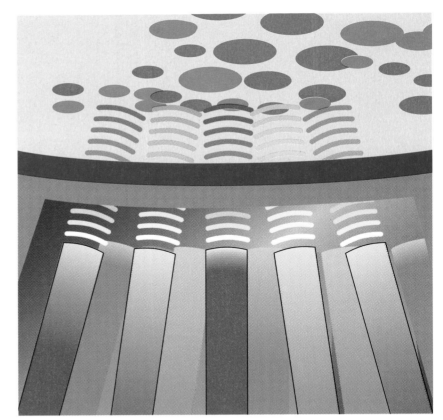

You can always tell when a color photo is printed by computer, right? It's got this crude look made up of hundreds of dots of color. You see what makes up the picture as much as you notice the subject matter of the photo. Or that's the way it used to be. Now a process called dye sublimation—also called dye diffusion thermal transfer (D2T2)—brings color computer printing to the level of photos fresh from the drug store. Dye sublimation produces *continuous-tone* printing. That means shades of color blend seamlessly to the naked eye. There are no thick bands of the same color in a limited number of shades to simulate color blending. There's none of the dithering that mixes color in clumsy clumps. A dye-sub printout is virtually indistinguishable from a color photograph.

So this must be a super-high resolution printer, right? Nope. It has a resolution of only 300 dots per inch (dpi), the same as the original laser printers. But the only place in which the 300dpi resolution jumps out at you is when an image includes straight, abrupt demarcations as in the case of text. The reason dye-sub hard copy looks so photographic in continuous-tone areas isn't because a dye-sublimation printer puts more dots on a page; it's because the printer varies the size of the dots to any of more than 200 measurements. The results are spectacular.

In fact, some professional photo finishers use dye-sub printers to produce oversized enlargements of pictures and posters. A dye-sub printer costs several thousand dollars, making it impractical for everyday printing. But it is perfect for business presentations and printing proofs, where the results are important enough to justify the price.

Dye-Sublimation Color Printer

1 A dye-sublimation printer uses a paper specially made to accept the printer's colors. A sheet of the paper is clamped to a drum to ensure that all the colors, which are applied in separate passes, precisely line up with each other.

4 After the dye for one color has been transferred to the paper, the drum reverses direction, returning the paper to its start position. Then the process repeats itself using a different color. This procedure is repeated until dye from all four bands of color have been applied to the paper.

2 As the drum turns, other gears in the printer turn a transfer roll of plastic film. The film—the equivalent of a ribbon in other printers—contains cyan (blue), magenta (red), yellow, and black dyes in bands the same width and height as the sheet of paper. Moving at the same speed as the surface of the drum holding the paper, the film passes along the surface of the paper.

3 At the point where the transfer roll is nearest the surface of the paper, thousands of heating elements cause the dye to *sublimate*—a scientific term for a solid melting to a gas without going through an intervening liquid stage. The gaseous dye is absorbed into the fiber of the paper.

5 Each of the heating elements produces any of 256 different temperatures. The hotter the temperature, the more dye is sublimated and transferred to the paper, producing a different shade of the dye's color. In effect, this gives the dye-sublimation printer the ability to create 16 million colors without resorting to the dithering used by other printers to mix colors.

360 percent enlargement of thermal wax transfer hard copy.

360 percent enlargement of dye-sublimation hard copy.

6 Sublimation also accounts for the resolution looking higher than 300dpi. Although a dye-sublimation printer may produce only 300 dots per inch, unlike a thermal wax transfer printer at 300dpi, the dots are not all the same size. A heating element that has a cooler temperature produces a smaller dot than a heating element with a hotter temperature. The result is that the apparent resolution of the hard copy is of photographic quality.

INDEX

PLEASE TAPE HERE ONLY—DO NOT STAPLE

6. What is your level of experience with personal computers? With the subject of this book?

	With PCs	With subject of book
Beginner...............	☐ -1 (24)	☐ -1 (25)
Intermediate...........	☐ -2	☐ -2
Advanced..............	☐ -3	☐ -3

7. Which of the following best describes your job title?

Officer (CEO/President/VP/owner)........ ☐ -1 (26)
Director/head........................ ☐ -2
Manager/supervisor................... ☐ -3
Administration/staff.................. ☐ -4
Teacher/educator/trainer.............. ☐ -5
Lawyer/doctor/medical professional....... ☐ -6
Engineer/technician................... ☐ -7
Consultant.......................... ☐ -8
Not employed/student/retired........... ☐ -9
Other (Please specify): _____ ☐ -0

8. What is your age?

Under 20............................. ☐ -1 (27)
21-29............................... ☐ -2
30-39............................... ☐ -3
40-49............................... ☐ -4
50-59............................... ☐ -5
60 or over.......................... ☐ -6

9. Are you:

Male............................... ☐ -1 (28)
Female............................. ☐ -2

Thank you for your assistance with this important information! Please write your address below to receive our free catalog.

Name: _____

Address: _____

City/State/Zip: _____

Fold here to mail.   344X-13-08

_____

_____

_____

BUSINESS REPLY MAIL
FIRST CLASS MAIL   PERMIT NO. 1612   OAKLAND, CA

POSTAGE WILL BE PAID BY ADDRESSEE

Ziff-Davis Press
5903 Christie Avenue
Emeryville, CA 94608-1925
Attn: Marketing

NO POSTAGE
NECESSARY
IF MAILED IN
THE UNITED
STATES

Ziff-Davis Press Survey of Readers

Please help us in our effort to produce the best books on personal computing.
For your assistance, we would be pleased to send you a FREE catalog
featuring the complete line of Ziff-Davis Press books.

1. How did you first learn about this book?

Recommended by a friend . . . . ☐ -1 (5)

Recommended by store personnel . . . . ☐ -2

Saw in Ziff-Davis Press catalog . . . . ☐ -3

Received advertisement in the mail . . . . ☐ -4

Saw the book on bookshelf at store . . . . ☐ -5

Read book review in: _____ ☐ -6

Saw an advertisement in: _____ ☐ -7

Other (Please specify): _____ ☐ -8

2. Which THREE of the following factors most influenced your decision to purchase this book? (Please check up to THREE.)

Front or back cover information on book . . . ☐ -1 (6)

Logo of magazine affiliated with book . . . . . . ☐ -2

Special approach to the content . . . . ☐ -3

Completeness of content . . . . ☐ -4

Author's reputation. ☐ -5

Publisher's reputation . . . . ☐ -6

Book cover design or layout . . . . ☐ -7

Index or table of contents of book . . . . ☐ -8

Price of book . . . . ☐ -9

Special effects, graphics, illustrations . . . . . . ☐ -0

Other (Please specify): _____ ☐ -x

3. How many computer books have you purchased in the last six months? _____ (7-10)

4. On a scale of 1 to 5, where 5 is excellent, 4 is above average, 3 is average, 2 is below average, and 1 is poor, please rate each of the following aspects of this book below. (Please circle your answer.)

Depth/completeness of coverage 5 4 3 2 1 (11)
Organization of material 5 4 3 2 1 (12)
Ease of finding topic 5 4 3 2 1 (13)
Special features/time saving tips 5 4 3 2 1 (14)
Appropriate level of writing 5 4 3 2 1 (15)
Usefulness of table of contents 5 4 3 2 1 (16)
Usefulness of index 5 4 3 2 1 (17)
Usefulness of accompanying disk 5 4 3 2 1 (18)
Usefulness of illustrations/graphics 5 4 3 2 1 (19)
Cover design and attractiveness 5 4 3 2 1 (20)
Overall design and layout of book 5 4 3 2 1 (21)
Overall satisfaction with book 5 4 3 2 1 (22)

5. Which of the following computer publications do you read regularly; that is, 3 out of 4 issues?

Byte . . . . ☐ -1 (23)

Computer Shopper . . . . ☐ -2

Corporate Computing . . . . ☐ -3

Dr. Dobb's Journal . . . . ☐ -4

LAN Magazine . . . . ☐ -5

MacWEEK . . . . ☐ -6

MacUser . . . . ☐ -7

PC Computing . . . . ☐ -8

PC Magazine . . . . ☐ -9

PC WEEK . . . . ☐ -0

Windows Sources . . . . ☐ -x

Other (Please specify): _____ ☐ -y

Please turn page.

See.

It's that simple.

Just open these colorfully illustrated guide-books and watch the answers to your software questions unfold.

The HOW TO USE books from Ziff-Davis Press make comp-uting easy by presenting each task visually on two facing pages. You'll see what you want to achieve, and exactly how to achieve it.

There's no guess work. The HOW TO USE books are the affordable alternative for those of us who would rather let the computer do the work.

For more information call (800) 688-0448, ext. 253. For Corporate/ Government programs, call (800) 488-8741 ext. 297. For Education programs, call (800) 786-6541.

HOW TO USE
Windows 95

ISBN: 1-56276-268-0
Price: $19.95

HOW TO USE
America Online

ISBN: 1-56276-349-0
Price: $19.95

HOW TO USE
The Internet

ISBN: 1-56276-348-2
Price: $19.95

ZIFF-DAVIS ZD PRESS

© 1995
Ziff-Davis Press